We Are Joy:

ReAwaken Your Joy

Mary Ann Pack

Envision Greatness Press

We Are Joy!: ReAwaken Your Joy
Copyright © 2022 Mary Ann Pack

All rights reserved. No part of this book may be used or reproduced by any means, graphic, electronic, or mechanical, including photocopying, recording, taping or by any information storage retrieval system without the written permission of the publisher, except in the case of brief quotations embodied in critical articles and reviews.

ISBN Paperback: 979-8-9854141-0-3

Cover design: Mary Ann Pack and Elizabeth B. Hill

This book is designed to provide information and motivation to our readers. It is sold with the understanding that the publisher is not engaged to render any type of psychological, legal, or any other kind of professional advice. The content of each article is the sole expression and opinion of its author, and not necessarily that of the publisher. No warranties or guarantees are expressed or implied by the publisher's choice to include any of the content in this volume. Neither the publisher nor the author shall be liable for any physical, psychological, emotional, financial, or commercial damages, including, but not limited to, special, incidental, consequential or other damages. Our views and rights are the same: You are responsible for your own choices, actions, and results.

Dedication

To all the indoctrinated souls who are re-membering all of their hidden, crushed, and closeted parts into wholeness.

To all the religious refugees who are on their path to becoming spiritual sovereigns.

To all the wise women who are awakening to their inner wisdom and voice.

To all the young women who are finding solace in the wisdom of the ancients.

I dedicate these words to you, not because you are broken or need to be fixed or saved, but because you simply need to be reminded who you really are as a goddess of joy embodied!

I am lovingly offering this message to you as I forge ahead of you to be a guiding light on the path to joyous wholeness!

You are joy!

We are joy!

Acknowledgments

We are not lone rangers. We are social beings and need a community for support and for our evolution. There are so many that have helped me on my path of transformation and I want to share my appreciation for some of those delightful folks!

First, I want to acknowledge my Collective Sisters. These are women that I have known from a year-long coaching program with our magical leader and mentor, Darla LeDoux. If it had not been for saying yes to the calling of my spirit to coach with Darla, I would have never met such amazing, supportive women. Thank you, Julie Flippin, for leading my personal coaching. Thank you to my Collective Sisters: Dr. Davia Shepherd, Lori Raggio, Robin Finney, Manda Stack, Meredith Vaish, Veronica Wirth, Sandy Tomey, Dr. Laura Monk, Olivia Florian, Wendy Lee, Akanke Rasheed, and Laura-Jean Anderson. Thank you for being my guides into all things life transformational!

Second, I want to acknowledge my editor and mentor, Elizabeth Hill of Green Heart Living Press. She held my hand and guided my steps in publishing this book. She is holding my vision with me of a series of these books!

Third, I want to acknowledge my mentor of many, many years, Abraham-Hicks. Listening to The Teachings of Abraham® through the voice of Esther Hicks has changed my life forever. I am eternally grateful.

Fourth, I want to acknowledge my own spirit guides, The

Many! They tried to introduce themselves to me in 2015 but I was much too afraid. When I was finally ready to reach out to them five years later, they graciously answered and we have been in conversation ever since.

Finally, I want to acknowledge my sweet partner and husband, Randy, for his support. His encouragement for me to write at every opportunity was his love gift of time and understanding. He listened to so many business ideas and simply kept asking me, *"What brings you joy? Do that!"*

So, here is the work that brings me joy!

Table of Contents

Foreword by Lori Raggio — 9

Introduction — 13

Chapter 1: Start with the Basics - We are Joy! — 15

Chapter 2: Selfishly Seek Joy! — 22

Chapter 3: How to Soothe Your Fear — 30

Chapter 4: Three Tips for Moving from Confusion to Clarity — 41

Chapter 5: People-Pleasing is Not Sustainable — 48

Chapter 6: Two Ways to Know What's Active in Your Vibration — 59

Chapter 7: Thieves of Joy — 69

Chapter 8: How to Move into Joy When You're Just Not Feeling It — 79

Chapter 9: Know Who You Really Are — 94

Chapter 10: Have a Great Day (Unless You've Made Other Plans) — 104

Chapter 11: Your Goal? Feel Good! — 110

Chapter 12: Feel Better First! — 117

Foreword

Mary Ann said with a huge smile, honest eyes and compelling soft voice, *"The Many have a message for you regarding your question about potential negative energy coming from the diamond earrings that were your mom's. They want you to know that diamonds are a symbol of love, purity and they bond relationships. They are amplifiers of energy and one of the few stones that do not need recharging. They impart fearlessness, invincibility, fortitude, and they aid in enlightenment. Any negative energy associated with your mom dissipated at the time of her moving from an earthly being to a spiritual being."* On numerous occasions, I have been a recipient of the powerful, transformational messages from Mary Ann's spirit guides, The Many. Their messages consistently leave me with a feeling of intense joy.

Mary Ann Pack models how to channel the frustration and challenge of misalignment into joy. She listened to her heart and soul which led her to be the joyous person she is and to use her powerful voice to tell her story and to support others' transformation. Mary Ann is the queen of joy. Once she learned to surrender to love and heart and soul alignment and allow herself to return to her birthright of joy she began a devotion to daily writing.

I met Mary Ann about three years ago when we both joined a transformational retreat leader certification program with our mentor Darla LeDoux, founder of Sourced™. We have continued to support each other's businesses and transformation and to live a sourced joyous life as we use our gifts to transform the world. I have witnessed Mary Ann on numerous occasions utilizing the magic of her expression and recognition to support others' transformation.

Joy is the most magnetic force in the universe. Joy is a net of love by which you can catch souls. Once you allow joy to be your focus you can live at your highest vibrational energy. Joy is based on what is happening within us, not on external factors. Joy is about helping us to co-create in community a new humanity which is so critical now.

Joy brings a feeling of elation, abundance, delight, exuberance, peace, and trust. Joy is the sunshine of the soul.

When I show up in my essence of Harmony, Power, Glow, Source, and Heart I can eliminate fear and accept trust, surrender, intuition, and clarity alignment. Joy can be reclaimed once we remove our armor and show up as our unique authentic self. I find my joy by feeding my inner child by bringing a childlike wonder lens to my life.

Joy is accessible when we give ourselves permission to be human with all of our idiosyncrasies. This is spiritual work that supports our energy in being expressed.

This book is thought-provoking and filled with concrete ways to move beyond our fear and comfort zones and to embrace our joy. Each of the twelve chapters includes a list of journal prompts to help support the integration of what has been learned.

In this book, Mary Ann, and her spirit guides, The Many, teach us to own our gifts and to allow our joy to seep through every cell of our being.

What gifts do you have pent up that are almost exploding to be expressed? What might be available if by expressing these gifts you can impact others and co-create a more joyous world?

The answers await you as you explore the pages of this book - and the series of books that will follow.

Lori Raggio

Lori Raggio, MBA, founder and CEO of Inspire Greatness Coaching and Consulting LLC, serves as the creation catalyst, soul activist and intuitive transformation alchemist helping women leaders and entrepreneurs remove their armor, find their authentic self, and live aligned with their passion and purpose.

She is a compassionate, innovative, strategic, and results-oriented leadership coach, human capital consultant, transformational retreat leader, best-selling author, and a geographical soulmate matchmaker. Lori is powered by purpose, driven by insatiable curiosity, and guided by Source to partner with women leaders to explore who they are courageously becoming and support them to intentionally impact the world by leveraging their talents and gifts in alignment with their heart and soul.

Introduction

Welcome home!

We love the idea that "home" should be comforting, loving, understanding, and accepting. Whether or not we actually experienced this in our home, that's what we envision a home should feel like.

Many people who visit my home comment that it is so comfortable and peaceful. They can relax and just be themselves. This thrills my heart!

It wasn't always this way. For many years, my home was full of tension and anger. I was not a person you'd want to be around because I was the queen of complaining! I possessed a very negative attitude which, in turn, my body was responding to in kind with dis-ease and pain.

When I crashed in 1993 at the age of 34 from all the drugs and surgeries, I knew I wouldn't see my 40th birthday if I didn't change my life. So, I asked for help from an owner of a health food store who set me on my path to wellness!

Seeking alternative healing allowed me to begin examining my beliefs. I realized so many of my beliefs were simply indoctrination from my religion and didn't resonate with my soul. So, it took years to come to the awareness that my beliefs had to change to live a life of thriving. I left the church in my mid-40s and have been thriving ever since. My well-being has returned and I'm happy and in joy!

Now, I want to share the message that we are joy embodied! I know folks are searching for more from life and crave happiness. As we remember who we really are as extensions of Source Energy, we will reawaken the joy that we truly are!

In the pages of this book, I hope you can feel my joy, comfort, love, understanding, and acceptance of who you really are. I hope you feel like you're home! The kind of home we all dream about!

This is the first of many books in a series with 12 lessons each with exercises to help you integrate what you'll be learning. You may hear some new perspectives or you may know much of what I teach in these lessons and it will be a good refresher. Many of the exercises will be similar or repeated because we learn by repetition.

In all cases, if you will read one lesson a week and follow the integrative practices during that week, you will have accomplished a lot of transformation in your life in three months. It will be like coaching with me during that time!

Visit WeAreJoyBook.com for all the books in the series as they launch and the book study membership with coaching and Q&As!

Chapter 1

Start with the Basics - We Are Joy!

You may be new to the knowledge of who you really are as joy, so welcome! In this first lesson, we will discover who you really are and why it matters for living your optimal life of thriving. This is the foundational premise to set you on your path for truly *knowing* that you are joy!

If you take anything from today's lesson, let it be this:

YOU ARE JOY - no matter what anyone has told you or the lies others have taught you to believe about who you are!

Ugh! How am I supposed to believe that I am joy? I don't feel that's who I am.

I've always been told I'm not good or even that I'm innately sinful! And, I must be because I do too many bad things; things I regret. And, don't forget about all the bad stuff people do to me or each other!!

It seems that no one is living a truly joy-filled life.

I do know I want to feel better and live a better life. I'd love to begin believing that I am joy and live like I know that's who I am without a shadow of a doubt!

I hear ya! I feel ya! I get it. I've muttered every one of these, if not screamed them, and occasionally still think about them! How can we be joy when there's so much going *wrong* in the world? If we were really joy, everyone would get along and do good things, right?

Here's the deal.

Our Inner Being, our soul or spirit, is JOY living in our body. How can I make that statement? Because our Inner Beings came from Source Energy (my name for God) and will return to Source. This is the eternal, older, wiser, non-physical part of us that is an extension of Source Energy.

Our Inner Being is that which IS Source (God). We are the stream of consciousness of pure love and well-being living in our physical bodies. It's our mind-body that can get out of alignment with the joy of who we really are!

Since we have chosen to come into this physical realm, we are governed by the Universal Laws. We will focus primarily on the Law of Attraction (LOA) for the purpose of understanding how to create our lives filled with joy and joyous experiences!

So, let's get started...

The premise of the Law of Attraction is *that which is like unto itself is drawn*. We understand that like attracts like. So, what is the *like* that is attracting to itself?

Like vibrations attract one another!

We live in a Universe that is vibrationally based. As a matter of fact, the Universe's language is that of vibration. So, everything we think and feel is the vibrational instructions to the Universe to essentially match and bring us more. The mantra of the Universe is MORE!

If you're wanting to create your own reality, what are the basics for doing that?

First of all, we do have to understand and acknowledge that our Inner Beings are pure positive love and joy, as an extension of Source Energy. Then, we must understand the laws by which our lives are governed so that we have the opportunity to create amazing realities!

We must understand that it's all about energy, frequencies, and vibrations. We are masters of receiving, interpreting, and emanating energetic vibrations. We interpret vibrations so well that we don't even realize we are doing it!

Every time we see, hear, smell, taste, and touch something, we are interpreting vibrations. Every time we think a thought or experience an emotion, we are vibrating. Even our bodies are vibrating - every cell has its own signature vibrational frequency!

When we think thoughts they elicit an emotional response in us. We can *feel* when we're feeling good and feeling bad or feeling positive and negative emotions. Our choice of thoughts created those emotions that are vibrating into the Universe as instructions for the Universe to bring us more feelings that match those.

So, maybe you can see where I'm going here. If we choose thoughts that feel good (positive) we are requesting the Universe to bring us more experiences that match those feelings. If we choose thoughts that feel bad (negative) we are requesting the Universe to bring us more experiences that match those feelings.

Yikes! How can I only keep my thoughts on things that feel good to get more good-feeling experiences?

You must choose to believe that you truly are joy embodied! It all begins with remembering who you really are. Because if you don't remember who you really are, as joy, nothing else makes any difference. You won't have a firm foundation for moving forward into your joy-filled life.

We must remember we are joy because we knew who we were when we came into this physical life. We remembered that we were Source Energy in the flesh. That we could be, do, and have anything we desired in this life.

When we start living life, we get indoctrinated into beliefs that don't really serve us and we forget who we are. We begin to believe lies that we're not good enough to live really joyful lives. Now, we're stuck believing lies about ourselves.

What's a belief anyway?! And, how the heck do I change my beliefs to be the joy I want to be?

I'm so glad you asked! A belief is only a thought we repeat to ourselves until we believe it is true - so, it eventually becomes our belief. If we believe that we are anything less than worthy and joyful, we have been taught to believe a lie.

When you begin to really believe that you are JOY emanating from Source Itself, that gives you amazing feelings of empowerment, confidence, clarity, freedom, and well-being. You begin to *believe* in yourself and trust the Universal Laws to be your dearest friends that assist you in creating your life of joy.

As you begin to repeat thoughts of being love, joy, freedom, peace, clarity, all-knowledge, and well-being - maybe as I AM statements - you will eventually believe strongly in your own Truth of being JOY!

"You are joy looking for a way to express. It's not just that your purpose is joy, it is that you are joy. You are love and joy and freedom and clarity expressing. Energy, frolicking and eager, that's who you are. And, so, if you're always reaching for alignment with that, you're always on your path, and your path will take you into all kinds of places. You are Pure Positive Energy that translates into the human emotion of joy."
~Abraham-Hicks

Do you not just get shivers of excitement in your soul and body when you read this truth?

I wanted to leave you with this quote because it made such an impact on my transformation. I was taught in my religion and home that I was innately sinful and unworthy. That I was so bad that I needed to be saved and obey dogmatic rules to be worthy enough to get into heaven and be accepted and loved by God.

So, when I read this quote for the first time, my heart jumped for joy! I felt that surge of joy race through my soul and my body. My Inner Being recognized Itself in the words. My body, physically, shouted for joy! In unison, my cells declared, *"Finally, she's recognizing herself as joy - who we really are!"*

To realize that joy is our life's purpose, yes! But, more importantly, that we *are* joy! Now, we can proclaim it from the rooftops!

WE ARE JOY EMBODIED!!!

Integrative Exercises

Use the following writing prompts this week to help you integrate what you've learned for your transformation.

This is a long list of suggestions, so you may want to pick a few to do this week that resonate most with where you are right now.

What makes you really joyful? Make a list of things that make you joyful and keep adding to it daily. When we do things that are joyful, we are aligned with our Inner Being. We are doing things that are true to who we are at the core of our Being.

Make it a point to do one or two of those things on your list of what makes you full of joy every day this week. *(Bonus Exercise: Do this for the rest of your life!)*

Write about the joyful things you've chosen to do each day. What did you do? What did you think about it? Describe how it made you feel. Were others involved?

Did your feeling of joy expand into your day and make it even better? Ask yourself this question each day this week and write about your experience, dance it out, sing, or describe it with art!

Where do you feel joy in your body? When you set your intention to do something joyful or think more joyful thoughts, notice where you feel it in your body. How does it feel? Does it have a color, make a sound, have a fragrance? Is it like chill-bumps? Does it make you want to shout, sing, dance, or create artwork? Write about this so you can become aware of how joy feels in your body.

Write an affirmation about being joy embodied and post it where you can read it every day. Or, you may want to begin an I AM affirmation journal. Write I AM statements every day. This practice will shift your beliefs. Remember, thoughts that you repeat to yourself *become* your beliefs - choose beliefs about being JOY!!

Hint: To help you ease into your I AM statements, you may need to use some bridging words such as begin/beginning, becoming, aware, learning, so that it's easier to begin creating your new beliefs about who you are. (Example: *I AM beginning to believe that I am joy embodied. I AM becoming more aware that I am clarity and freedom at the core of my being. I AM learning to trust that I truly am love and well-being.*)

Chapter 2

Selfishly Seek Joy!

"Selfishly seek joy because joy is the greatest gift you can give anyone! Unless you are in your joy, you have nothing to give anyway!"
~Abraham-Hicks

How does this quote make you feel? Does it make you feel uncomfortable to think about being selfish?

What do you believe about being selfish?

Were you taught that it's not good to be selfish? That you should always put others' desires and wishes above your own? That putting yourself first was bad or even evil?

Understand this, we cannot get away from being selfish. We only have a "self" perspective. We don't have an "other" perspective. Only we can perceive what we experience in the "self." If we declare "self" to be wrong or evil, we are condemning who we really are! We are condemning Source Energy because we are THE extension of Source embodied!! Source cannot declare Itself evil.

There are two ways to perceive being selfish.

One is that being selfish is bad, wrong, maybe even sinful. That we are here to put others first. To serve others first no matter how it makes us feel. To sacrifice our happiness and joy because it is our duty and responsibility to please others. And, this unsustainable selfishness is deemed to be good!

The second is to be so devoted to yourself that you make feeling joy your number one priority because that is the indication that you are in alignment with your Inner Source. In this way, you will be available to be of benefit to others in your joy! But, this selfishness is deemed wrong?!

What is the underlying motivation for implying that being selfish is bad or wrong?

I believe the teaching that selfishness for feeling good and putting our joy first being wrong comes from those who are out of alignment with their own Inner Source. They are not truly in touch with their own higher "Self." They don't want *you* to be selfish and think of what pleases you first because they selfishly want you to please them! If you are selfishly feeling good, you won't be in a position to please them on their terms.

If you are selfish enough to make feeling good your number one priority, it may take away from doing or being the way the other person demands. This is conditional selfishness.

Please me, not yourself.

Do this or be this way because that's the only way I'll feel better.

It is your responsibility to make me feel better so don't be so selfish about your time, money, and energy.

People who demand that others please them are actually giving away their power for happiness.

When you allow someone to be responsible for your happiness you are totally disempowered to live a happy life on your own. The underlying dysfunction is that those who don't want us to be selfish are because they are truly selfishly, egotistically demanding we serve them above ourselves. They are demanding that we need to do for them what they don't want to be responsible for in themselves - to be happy and live in joy.

This is conditional selfishness. We don't like our condition and don't want to take responsibility for our condition. We want others to be different, act different, to make our condition different, so we can feel better.

When I was a kid at church, we were taught that JOY meant Jesus-Others-You. You were to put everyone else above yourself. You were to think about yourself last. Your needs or desires were not as important as the duty to serve others. I don't believe that way anymore. I'll tell you why a little later.

What is the underlying inspiration for implying that being selfish is good and beneficial for all?

The truth is, if we would all be selfish enough to seek our own joy first and foremost, that would leave everyone else off the hook for doing or being different to make us feel better! The condition would be non-existent. We would feel better no matter the condition.

No one would have to jump through our hoops to make us feel better. We would feel better first on our own; under our own empowerment. And, what the other person(s) did or didn't do wouldn't matter to us at all. Everyone would be free to live their lives in alignment and joyful in their souls where we could not do anyone else harm.

Feeling better, feeling joy, is an inside job for each of us.

No one is responsible for our joy or happiness except us. When we hold someone else responsible for our happiness and require them to change who they are to fit into our demands, we are totally being selfish in an egotistical manner, and not in a beneficial way for anyone involved.

We should be so devoted to ourselves that we seek joy for ourselves first.

We should be so loyal, loving, and enthusiastic about our joy that we overflow with joy toward others. Others around us would benefit from being in our energetic space. They would feel better just by being near us. Our joyful presence would be a healing balm!

We would also be able to lend a helping hand or be of service to others from a place of joy and satisfaction, instead of sacrifice and duty. This attitude shift would be amazingly beneficial. This is pure alignment with our Inner Source - who we really are - who we intended to be as we came into this life.

When we are in our own joy, we won't see people as needy or needing to be fixed because we won't see them as broken.

We would see them through the eyes of Source, as whole and eternally loving beings of light. Fully capable of everything they desire once they are aligned with their own Inner Source. We would allow them to do for themselves what they deeply know they want to do. We would no longer do for them the things they are responsible for.

We would no longer disempower them with the attitude that they can't do this work on their own - they can't be happy or in joy on their own without our assistance. As if we must do it for them. That attitude is so disempowering for them.

We must allow each person to selfishly choose, yes *selfishly* choose, to seek their own happiness and joy!

That means us, too!

When we each selfishly seek our joy, we are giving others the best of ourselves! OUR joy is the greatest gift we can give anyone. If we're not in our own joy, we have nothing to give.

If our joy-cup is empty or even running low, we have no surplus to give away. We must fill our joy-cup first to be able to serve with joy. We can be happy doing things for others, not from sacrifice, but from joy! We will serve others because we truly love serving!

Now I believe JOY to mean, Joyously Opening Yourself!

This resonates with my soul so much more than what I was taught JOY to mean as a child. As I am joyously open to myself, I have a greater opportunity to be joyously open to serving, also! I see everyone as the joyous soul they *are* no matter what they are doing, being, or saying. My love for them doesn't have to be conditional any more. I can love just because I AM LOVE! AND, I know that in their soul, THEY ARE LOVE!

I know I cannot feel hate, disdain, or be critical of anyone and feel love at the same time. It's impossible. It's also impossible to feel that someone is broken or needs to be fixed by me and then think I'm going to help and serve from an attitude of pure joy because joy only sees us all as powerful creators of joy. These kinds of emotions are on diametrically opposing frequencies.

If I'm irritated or frustrated with someone, or I'm doing something for them out of an attitude of obligation or duty from sacrificing, I'm not really serving them nor myself. This attitude builds resentment in both of us. Resentment for me that I'm having to do this thing that I don't want to do and resentment for them because I can't do it *right* or I can't do enough to satisfy them. When, in fact, we are both simply out of alignment at that moment and we must do the inside work for ourselves but are refusing to take our own responsibilities.

So, really, we do ourselves and everyone else a great disservice if we are not selfish enough to take care of our own alignment, first. To care so much about how we feel that we make feeling good our number one priority because we know that is living in an aligned state of being. That we care so much about our alignment, we are consistently more in the receiving mode of joy.

As we receive more joy in ourselves, we will naturally transmit that joyous energy into our world. We will be of greatest influence because that's the energy that precedes us wherever we go. We are actually pre-paving our energetic path to receive more joy from new experiences and rendezvous with people we encounter.

So, it's time to selfishly seek joy!

If we want joy, and I'm sure you do or you wouldn't have chosen this book, we have to selfishly care about our alignment because that's the only place that joy resides. Love, joy, and appreciation are the vibrational essence of that which is Source Energy. And, since we ARE extensions of that Source, we are inherently love, joy, and appreciation!

If we don't live in joy, we are not living authentically who we really are!

Go be selfish enough that you seek joy. Covet joy. Nurture joy in yourself. Then, go spread that shit everywhere!

Integrative Exercises

Use the following writing prompts this week to help you integrate what you've learned for your transformation.

What do you believe about being selfish enough to seek your own joy? Did you experience a new perspective about what it means to be selfish?

Where do you need to allow yourself to be more selfish?

Where can you allow others to take more responsibility for their own joy and happiness as you've begun to understand their happiness is not dependent upon you?

How are you overextending and over-giving in sacrifice and duty for others?

How can you lovingly say no to someone who is demanding too much from you?

In what new ways can you selfishly set aside time for yourself to focus on your joy and happiness? This may be a 5-10 minute practice of writing about what brings you the most joy or even writing a list of things you appreciate. You may even want to express your joy and happiness in movement, music, or art. Remember, joy and appreciation are the vibrational essences of Source, so when you attain that state of being, you are in pure alignment!

How can you move into practicing more Joyously Opening Yourself? What does this look like to you? What does that feel like? What can you create by practicing JOY?

What will the allowing of your joy to be your priority make available for you that was not previously available as you lived in sacrifice and duty by over-giving? Will it feel like freedom? What does freedom feel like?

Chapter 3

How to Soothe Your Fear

We all suffer from the feeling of fear from time to time. Usually, it comes and is reconciled pretty quickly. Right now with all the chaos in the medical, economic, and political arenas, fear-mongering is in full swing. It's when we suffer from chronic fear that fear causes us problems.

Today, we'll discuss what fear is and how to soothe ourselves. We are here to thrive joyously in all conditions, but when we continue to live in fear it diminishes our joy and wreaks havoc in our health, relationships, finances, and spirituality.

Let's begin with a clear understanding of who we are and how the Universe works.

We must understand that we are more than just our physical mind-body. We are, also, a spirit or an Inner Source that is an eternal being of pure light and love. It is our work to blend into the wholeness of who we really are. That means knowing, thinking, and feeling like our Inner Being - which always feels really good. As we align and blend spirit-mind-body we are the wholeness of what we intended when we came into this life. That is coherence. That is alignment.

We must, also, understand that this Universe is governed by vibration. The language of the Universe is vibration. So, as the Law of Attraction causes like vibrations to attract, it is the vibration of our thoughts and feelings that attract our life experiences. Our vibrational thoughts and emotions equal our point of attraction.

Our Inner Source also has a point of attraction which is always feeling good. When we can blend our mind-body's point of attraction with our Inner Being's point of attraction, then we have powerfully focused energy attracting what we desire and deserve!

Finally, we must understand that our emotions tell on our thoughts every single time. Our emotions are indicators of the direction we are heading toward wanted or unwanted experiences. This is our wonderful emotional guidance system that can be trusted in every instance. By noticing how we feel, we'll know our direction. And, if we don't like our direction, we can change our thoughts to those that feel better and return to the direction of what we want.

It is imperative to understand these premises for the rest of this lesson to make sense. I'm glad you're taking the time to read and understand for your highest benefit!

What is fear and what is it telling us?

In this lesson, I'm not referring to the fear from our amygdala - the fight-flight-freeze type of survival fear. That type of fear is for our protection during times of imminent danger. Once the danger passes, our bodies return to homeostasis.

In this lesson, I'm referring to the fear that is sustained over long periods of time from constant stress, whether of real or perceived danger. It's usually about something we fear that may or may not happen in the future. This fear is typically future-oriented. Living in this type of fear is playing the what-if game from a negative perspective as we project our thoughts of what may happen in the future.

Fear is an emotion that indicates our resistance.

We are creating contradictory energy because of our thoughts. Our Source Energy vibrates at a high frequency that can be interpreted as the human emotions of love, joy, appreciation, clarity, and well-being. When we are in a state of love, joy, and appreciation, we are essentially aligned with our Inner Source - we are One. And, fear is not an issue because we feel no undue stress. We are relaxed and at peace with our future even if it is unknown and uncertain.

When we experience fear, we are thinking and feeling in opposition to what our Inner Source is knowing, thinking, and feeling about the subject we are focused on. We know this because we feel so bad. Fear feels really bad. In that low vibration, we are not aligned with our Inner Being! We feel the discord of our misalignment.

Do you know why we feel that discord? It's because our Inner Being is NOT ever feeling fear and is ALWAYS feeling confidence, security, safety, peace, well-being, ease, and trust. So, you can *know* when you feel fear, your Inner Being is feeling really good!

All negative emotion is from thinking in opposition to who we really ARE. Our fear is based on thoughts that our Inner Being is *not* thinking - so, we feel how distant we are from what our Inner Being is thinking at that moment.

"Fear is the perception of a lack of freedom. You're thinking something has power, that wishes you harm, that can affect you in some negative way and you have no way of controlling it." ~Abraham-Hicks

Fear is not about what IS happening, it's about our PERCEPTION of what is happening. We are perceiving that our freedom is lacking - that we have no choices. We are perceiving that whatever we are focused on is taking away our freedom, intending us harm, causing us to feel bad.

But, it's not that thing or person that causes us to feel fear, it's our thoughts *about* a perceived lack of freedom. It's always about our thoughts. At times, we may feel that some of our freedoms have been taken away from us, but our freedom of thought can never be taken from us!

If we were vibrational matches to what our Inner Beings were thinking, we would feel amazingly free even through any

perceived chaos! We would never be frightened by anything or anyone. We would understand that we have control of our vibration by choosing our thoughts - ones that match our Inner Source who knows we are safe and free.

Our feeling of fear is telling us that our emotional guidance system is working perfectly! Fear feels horrible, so that indicates we are thinking far from what our Inner Source's opinion is about any subject we're contemplating. Again, our Inner Source is never fearful and is always feeling good!

How do we get fearful?

We touched on the kinds of fear earlier, but let's distinguish between the two types of fear. The first fear is our innate fear, our primal fear of fight-flight-freeze. That fear is there to protect us from imminent danger to help us run away, dodge, or freeze in place. That is our ancestral fear for our physical protection.

The second type of fear is rooted in our thoughts, worries, frustration, what-if this is not safe, or that doesn't work out well. Fear from the unknown or uncertainty. This is the fear that creates stress in our bodies and doesn't leave because we keep this pattern of thought going endlessly, sometimes.

So many teachers and coaches say that this fear is an innate human trait, something that is born within us. I have to throw the BS card on that. To me, that is a false premise. Here's why....

I believe we are born with our all-knowing, vibrational non-physical part of us intact and fully functioning in alignment with our mind-body. We know we create our own realities by how we vibrate (how we feel). Even though babies have no spoken language, they are creating their reality all the time by letting the parents know what they like and dislike, what they want and don't want by expressing their emotions! They are certainly communicating by their vibrational offering loud and clear!

Fear is a learned trait. We did not come into this world with this type of fear. This fear is a practiced belief. We think patterns of thought of worry, doubt, and negative what-ifs until we *believe* they are true. Then, we end up looking for evidence that they are true and the Universe obliges us with proof because we have focused so strongly. However, we can deactivate fear by reawakening what we've always known since before we came into this physical life: that all is well!

We learn to be fearful by listening to others' opinions, from their place of misalignment with their Inner Beings. We cannot feel fear and love at the same time! It's impossible. They are miles apart vibrationally.

One is caused by high vibrational, good feeling thoughts that are in alignment with our Inner Source (love), and the other is caused by low vibrational, bad feeling thoughts that are in opposition to what our Inner Being is thinking at the exact same moment (fear).

As a side note: Don't confuse fearful worry about someone with love! Being fearful or worried about someone is about as far as you can get from true unconditional love. When you love, you love freely without any worry about their future. You place no condition on their outcome and let them live their life with their Inner Being's guidance whether they choose to accept it or not. You simply love because you are love.

We've listened to others who believed that outside forces can affect them adversely. They believe others can assert things into their lives against their will. They believe people can do unwanted things TO them. They believe they have no control over what germs get them next. They believe growing old means getting sick and declining. They've repeated those thoughts to themselves until they become beliefs. As their beliefs continued, they looked for proof of the truth of their beliefs, and, low and behold, the Universe obliged them with the evidence they were seeking.

Yet, someone else experiencing the same incidents can have totally different responses. They may see whatever makes you fearful as some wonderful opportunity! They may see its value and positive aspects, knowing that everything is working out for them. They trust that all is well and they are at peace. No stress, no fear!

And, when they look for the evidence that all is well, the Universe will oblige them and send them the proof they are looking for! It's all about our perception and what we're focused on finding and searching for evidence to prove we were right to believe what we believe. Belief is in the eye of the beholder.

The Universe doesn't care what you're thinking, it's consistently matching vibrations. It simply responds to the vibration of thoughts and emotions. It's up to *you* to choose what vibrational signals you are sending into the Universe to match.

Fear is resistance. Resistance to knowing and trusting who you really are. Fear is resisting your Inner Being's guidance. You get fearful when you think in opposition to what your Inner Being knows, thinks, and feels about you and about any given situation - even the fearful ones!

Prolonged resistance that causes fear will begin to take its toll on your health, your finances, your relationships, and most certainly your spirituality. Your body can only tolerate fear and stress for so long before it begins to break down and show signs of dis-ease (imbalance, uneasiness). When you don't feel good, emotionally and physically, it can put a strain on your relationships. You may feel so bad you can't even go to work - even when you work from home! Don't let fear ruin your life! You have the power within that you simply need to exercise. It's your thinking muscle!

Fear is you not looking forward to where your Inner Being is already. Fear is telling you there is energy moving because you're ready for a breakthrough!

Integrative Exercises

Use the following writing prompts this week to help you integrate what you've learned for your transformation.

How do you soothe your fears? Read the following suggested practices and as you apply any of them, write about how they help you soothe your fears. Which practices resonate most with you?

Remember who you really are as an extension of Source Energy. When you can grasp a hold of the power of who you really are, your fears will subside.

Stop talking about your fears and what makes you fearful. Thinking and talking about *any subject* that brings you to fear is activating the energy of it and the Universe will match you up with more of it. It's law. Stop giving your powerful attention to something you don't want to continue to attract. Change the subject!

Check in with yourself several times a day and notice how you're feeling. If you're feeling fearful, change the subject. Take a walk, play with your pet, or even take a nap!

What can you find to think about that feels better? Make a list of things you love and appreciate. Keep this list handy to read when you need to activate a new pattern of thought. Maybe it will include dancing, singing, listening to music, or an uplifting podcast. Maybe it's a wonderfully delightful memory or anticipating a party or fun vacation. If any thought feels better, you're heading in the right direction.

Focus on things you appreciate. Decide that you're going to change the subject and hold a good-feeling thought pattern long enough to allow the fear to diminish in power and strength. Activating patterns of thought about things that bring you pleasure will deactivate any subject you struggle with. Appreciation is the vibrational equivalent of Source Energy. Write a list of things you appreciate every day this week. If you're not a fan of writing, make your list by recording it in your voice recording app on your phone so you can listen anytime you need a lift. It's powerful to hear ourselves speaking love back to us!

Trust yourself to hear guidance from your Inner Being. Your Inner Being is always feeling good and is never fearful. Don't you think it's about time to make the decision that you're going to make feeling good your number one priority and trust that your Inner Being has your back at all times?

When you're feeling bad, ask your Inner Being, *"What do you know, think, and feel about me and about this situation?"* Then get quiet and spend some time listening to their answer and write down the message or even the feeling you receive. Did it feel like a relief?

Meditate and then listen for guidance or to receive inspired ideas or uplifting thoughts. When you quiet your mind in meditation, you are also quieting those fearful thoughts. In this non-resistant state, your vibration naturally rises. The better you feel, the higher the vibration. After meditation, sit with your journal and write down any thoughts or feelings that arise.

Be deliberate about what thoughts you think! When you sleep at night all momentum stops. That means every morning is a new day to choose your thoughts. Are you going to rehash yesterday's fears? Are you going to choose to think of things you appreciate? Don't allow yourself to get sloppy in your thinking. Keep your thoughts in alignment with your Inner Being and you will know you are there when you feel good. It's your choice!

How to plan for a great day! Before going to bed each night, think about things you appreciated during the day or things you are grateful for. Set the intention that you want peaceful sleep and to wake up refreshed and excited for the new day! In the morning, wake up and put a smile on your face and express your gratitude for a new day to live in appreciation and joy! Thank yourself for becoming more of who you really are - JOY! Carry this attitude throughout the day.

Chapter 4

Three Tips for Moving from Confusion to Clarity

Isn't it just the best thing ever when we experience clarity?!

Clarity feels so good!

Clarity feels like confidence, motion forward, inspiration, ease, and flow.

When we are clear-minded, our focus is laser-sharp. We can make decisions easily. It feels like we know exactly which direction to head that will be the most beneficial.

If we love clarity so much, why do we put up with confusion at all?

I believe it's because we aren't taking the time to prepare our energetic environment to receive clarity. Yes, I said *receive* clarity. Clarity is not something we conjure through hard work or effort. We can't force ourselves to be clear-minded because it's more than just about the mind. Clarity includes our intuition.

At the core of who we really are, we are clarity.

Clarity is an attribute of eternal Beings of Light and Love.

(*That's us!*) Our Inner Being always has clarity about what's important to us. Do you know why?

Our Inner Being *becomes* our desires immediately and has clarity about how to get us there.

Our Inner Being has clarity because we have put everything into our personal vortex of desires and our Inner Being has already *become* those desires. Our Inner Being is clear about who we really are, what we want, where it is, and how to get us there. We, the physical mind-body, are the ones who get confused! Our Inner Being, the eternal non-physical, always has clarity and never gets confused about anything, ever!

Once we align with our Inner Being, she is able to share with us what we already put into the vortex. She's simply reminding us of what we may have forgotten.

When we align, our Inner Being can remind us and give back to us what we've put there via thoughts, imagination, and daydreaming. So, we are able to receive the clarity that already exists within us!

Every time you set aside time to daydream or use your imagination about what you want, you don't conjure those thoughts. You actually receive them from your Inner Being. Our imagination is our Inner Being speaking to us and reminding us about what we've already said we want and then adding even more clarity to those thoughts.

Clarity has everything to do with alignment with who we really are as joy embodied!

So, how do we maintain a higher level of clarity?

What steps can we take to make clarity part of our everyday lives?

Here are three tips or processes you can use every day to gain more clarity in your life.

One: Meditate every day.

Quiet your mind. It's important to quiet your mind every day for 15-20 minutes. Especially at the beginning of the day when you've not been as exposed to as many resistant thoughts that come with engaging in daily life.

No distracting thoughts mean no resistant thoughts, so your vibration naturally rises. Your natural state of Being is that of well-being. When you quiet your thoughts, you also quiet your resistance which allows your natural level of high vibration to resume.

Listen for inspiration. Many times, during or after meditation, you will receive an inspired thought, a new thought, or a new idea that feels really good. It may be something really simple, but it feels like an impulse to go do something. Go. Do. That!

The more you follow those inspired impulses or ideas, the more you will feel the clarity that comes from allowing yourself to receive. Then, you may just start receiving new thoughts and ideas about the big stuff you really love!

Two: The COAT Method™

Chill Out And Trust! I received this acronym during meditation! So, I thought it would come in handy here as we are reaching for more clarity. When contrast shows us what we don't want (problem/confusion), we immediately know what we do want instead (solution/clarity). The problem and solution are created at the exact same moment!

But, so many times we are so focused on figuring out the problem - where it came from, who caused it, and when it will go away - that we lose sight of the solution. We throw up all kinds of obstacles on our paths by jumping into action way too soon! We are going to make something happen, by golly! If we would simply Chill Out And Trust, we would be in the mode of higher vibration to allow the solution to appear - the idea, the way, the light bulb of clarity!

Don't beat up on yourself when you have negative emotions. Negative feelings indicate that our emotional guidance system is working perfectly! They let us know that we are simply not thinking in alignment with our Inner Being. We feel the discordant vibration which we are feeling as a bad-feeling emotion.

Once we experience the negative feelings, it's time to acknowledge them, thank them, *(yes, thank them)*, and look to our Inner Being for clarity. Ask yourself: **What does my Inner Being know, think, and feel about me and about this situation?**

When you receive a thought after asking yourself that question if a thought feels good, you can be assured it is coming from your Inner Being. That will go a long way in soothing yourself AND bringing clarity to the situation!

Recognize that negative emotions are indicating that the problem just created a solution. When we experience a problem or contrast, it has been created on a low vibrational frequency. The solution, however, is immediately created and resides on a high vibrational frequency. You must choose which one you're going to focus on.

Three: Segment Intending

Segment intending is an awesome way to receive more clarity! A segment of your day is anytime you change from one situation to another. When you get up, that is a segment. When you leave the house to drive, that is another segment. When someone walks into the room, that is a different segment. If you have to make a call, that is still another segment.

The point of segment intending is to get clear about what you want to experience during this next segment. It is pre-paving the energy you want to project into the next segment to prepare and influence your next experience.

How to Segment Intend. Stop before you begin the next segment and ask yourself, **How do I want to feel? What do I want to experience in this segment?** And, list all the good-feeling experiences or emotions you'd enjoy experiencing. This is setting your intention with a strong emotional vibration into the Universe so they can match your desired intention!

Confusion diminishes and clarity becomes dominant. As your new clarity takes center stage, that old confusion will become a thing of the past. As long as you consciously take the time to segment intend and align with the feelings you want to experience, you can receive clarity. Segment intending takes practice and it is so worth it!

This week as you practice being a vessel for clarity, I hope you enjoy developing a deep and rich relationship with your Inner Being. Our Inner Beings are always in joy and calling us to live out our joy in these physical bodies!

Integrative Exercises

Do these three tips every day for the next week. It would be even better to do them for a full 30 days!

1) **Meditate Every Day.**
2) **Chill Out and Trust.**
3) **Segment Intending.**

If you need to, set alarms on your phone to remind you to begin these practices. Refer to the sections in this lesson to remember how to perform these.

Write about your experiences with each or pick one and write in your journal about your experience. Look for ways you can improve your practices. If you prefer expressing how this experience felt to you by moving your body with music, walking in nature, singing, or creating art, by all means go for it!

Chapter 5

People-Pleasing is Not Sustainable

"You can do 99 things for some people and all they will remember is the one thing you didn't do."
~PowerOfPositivity

People. Pleasing. Does. Not. Work!

It is not sustainable. People-pleasing was never meant to be a sustainable relationship. *Heck, it was never meant to be a part of any relationship!* It will wear you out and make you resentful and very unhappy. And, in the end, it will never really please the other person in the way they want to be pleased - all the time!

We are all here, physically, to experience a great relationship with Ourselves – the Non-physical (spiritual, eternal). When that relationship is not at its best, we look outside ourselves to shore up our desired feeling of alignment that we are missing. We look to others for our validation and value.

If we would look within, we would find it readily available at every moment. That outside-seeking is never going to satisfy our need for alignment within, so it will never please us and make us happy enough to live a joy-filled life. We will always feel dependent upon others to do the work we intended to perform within to gain our personal alignment with who we really are.

Please stop trying to please others at the risk of emotional, mental, and physical exhaustion on your part! It is futile.

None of us came into this physical life with the purpose to please others and make sure they were happy. Not even our parents, partners, or kids! *Oh my!* We came into this life with the express purpose of living joyful, creative lives. We *never* intended to be dependent on anyone else for our happiness or our alignment. Nor did we come to make everyone else happy at our expense.

That means...each of us! That doesn't mean *some* of us came to be pleased and *some* of us came to be pleasers! **We each came here knowing that it was solely our job to create our own happiness – without anyone else's help – or demanding anything from anyone.** No control. No demands. It's all an inside job for each person.

How do I know people-pleasing is hurtful?

I know because of how it makes me feel when I succumb to people-pleasing tactics. I feel like shit! When I get stuck doing something for someone that I never wanted to do in the first place, but did it anyway out of responsibility or obligation it never feels good. Even if it's someone I love and adore, there are just some folks that ask too much or ask too frequently. Or, I've been over-extending myself and really have no energy to do the favor at the time.

You know the feeling – you start to get tense, maybe your stomach churns or you get a lump in your throat. You start to resent having to do something, again, for this one who always seems to be so good at needing emergency help, or in-a-bind-favors. Over and over again. It gets very exhausting!

It makes you want to hold up the sign that reads, **"Your poor planning does not constitute an emergency on my part!"**

People-pleasing can adversely affect your health.

Besides your mental and emotional stress, all that tension and resentment is taking a toll on your physical body. Your body is very sensitive to the vibrational frequencies you are emitting through your thoughts and emotions.

If your emotions are out of whack – imagine what your poor body is going through! Pretty soon, you'll have a reason not to extend any more favors, because your body will create an illness, pain, or dis-ease that will prevent you from people-pleasing, anyway. Please don't wait that long. *I lived this sickly life for way too many years before reawakening my joy!*

When to say, yes, and when to say, no.

I'm NOT saying you can *never* do something for someone else. Not at all! If you can absolutely do something for another person as you stay aligned and happy in the doing of it – then by all means – follow your heart! It can be an amazing delight to be a help to another person!

I'm talking about the repetitive cries for help that never seem to end. Sometimes they tend to get bigger and more time-consuming. You'd like to tell them to get their shit together and get a life. They are not the center of your universe – you are!

If we feel taken advantage of, it's time to learn to set boundaries. Takers tend to step and stomp all over their helpers' lives. Taking no notice of the inconvenience and expense they may cause another.

Have you heard of boundaries?

I know, boundaries can be difficult to set and respect for yourself, when others give you that *look* or clear their throat in just that certain way. But, setting boundary lines is the only way to stop the abuse. And, yes, people-pleasing is abusive.

It's time to go within and see where we need to shift our thoughts and beliefs - and, maybe how we're treating ourselves. Setting boundaries is our opportunity to think different thoughts.

Did we attract these time and energy vampires?

Obviously, we have attracted the time- and energy-vampires by our previous vibrational thought patterns and beliefs. We invited people to demand our time and energy by thinking thoughts of our not enough-ness–that we *have* to serve and sacrifice ourselves for the good of others.

Toxic beliefs we may hold:

We hold beliefs that we must serve others *before* our own needs and desires are met.

That being selfish with my time and resources is wrong.

That it is better to give than receive!

Thinking, if I can just change my behavior enough to please him/her/them, then I will be appreciated and accepted.

Bullpucky!!

How do we know when it's time to be of assistance?

You can't keep serving from an empty cup. The cup is meant for your nourishment and sustenance. It's only when you are so fully aligned that your cup overflows into your saucer. The content of the saucer is available from which to serve others. Once that content in the saucer is gone, you cannot dip into your reserves for them!

You must fill yourself back up to overflowing into the saucer before you have something else to give anyone. That's why they tell you on airline flights to secure your oxygen mask *before* helping others. If you don't take care of your well-being *first*, you may be laying on the floor needing help yourself.

Self-care is necessary and life-sustaining.

Time and resources are solely ours to keep or share at our bidding. Giving and receiving are two sides of the exact same coin – they are equal! We can never change our behavior enough to please anyone for any length of time – because they are always changing what they want us to be or do, according to their whim of the day.

When someone is truly in need and we can feel good while we are performing the favor, then, by all means, do it! Delight in serving another. But, never, ever perform a favor for someone if you are doing it out of dread, fear, obligation, guilt, resentment – you get the picture.

In this attitude, you will not truly help them or yourself. Only perform favors when you are happy and truly glad to help out. Our alignment with who we really are is the guiding inspiration regarding any action to be performed. If it feels good – do it!

Focusing on their *need* compounds the energy surrounding their problem!

Another principle to follow is not to do something for someone with their *need* as your focus. Your focus on their problem or need only compounds their problem! So, in the long run, you are expanding more of the same kind of problem for them. You are basically saying to them, *"As I see you cannot do this for yourself, I will do it for you."* That attitude is so disempowering for them! That is such a destructive position for them and an ego trip for you.

They *want* to take responsibility for their own alignment. They came here to live a life in joy and satisfaction of a truly aligned life. When you disempower them by doing what you believe they cannot do for themselves, you are not helping them to take responsibility for their own inner work of developing a relationship with their Inner Being – who will guide them into better and better living.

View them as a whole being and fully capable of their own alignment!

Remember, anything you focus your attention on, by Law of Attraction, expands. You want to see them as whole and fully capable of aligning with their Inner Being. Do it, just because you see their amazing potential to live a fully aligned life. Then, you are seeing them through the eyes of Source! Then, you will make an impact for the good of all involved!

Looking inward: Are we the ones demanding that others please us?

On the other side of this, we may need to question if we are the person who is not appreciating the favors of time and energy someone has given us.

Are we the ones who constantly demand favors from others?

Are we the one who is not appreciating the 99 things people do for us and only remembering that one thing they didn't do?

Are we holding a grudge for that one little thing left undone?

If we are a time- and energy-vampire, it's time to focus upon our own alignment with our Inner Being and let go of the need to control others' behavior to make us feel better. Feeling better is truly what we are looking for – which only comes through our alignment with our Inner Source.

Maybe it's time to take up our own job of alignment with our Inner Being and begin thinking in new ways that help us feel better and better. Maybe it's time to change some beliefs – that others *owe* us, that we are the center of everyone's universe, that we are the victim and we can't help it, that everyone's out to get us, that we simply cannot help ourselves.

I totally relate to having been a people-pleaser. I could never make people happy enough, proud of me enough. I felt walked over and resentful. On the flip side, I was also the one demanding others to please me!

For many years, I was the one always needing the emergency favors. Over and over I would get myself into a jam and expect others to bail me out. Until I began to understand the principles of the Law of Attraction and the inner work I needed to do, my life was miserable and very sick.

I knew I wanted more from life but didn't know how to get there until I asked for guidance from mentors and coaches. Over the last two decades of learning about mindset and the quality of my thoughts, I can say I'm happy most of the time! And, that state of happiness has rewarded me with well-being! I began to look for things that were going right in my life – things I appreciated. I took my focus off of everything that was going wrong, being the past queen of complaining, and why I was the victim. Happy day!

Appreciation is always the key!

Look for things to appreciate. If someone is doing something for us, tell them how much we appreciate all their help. Make lists of things we appreciate about our life and the part others play in our experience. Look for positive aspects of all that comes our way.

The more we make the effort to live a life of appreciation, the more the universe feels this new shift in our vibration and will bring us more things to appreciate! **Remember and make a list of all the 99 things done for us. As we focus our appreciation on the 99 things, we'll not even remember the one that didn't get done.** It won't even matter when we live aligned as joy embodied!

Integrative Exercises

Use the following writing prompts this week to help you integrate what you've learned for your transformation.

Let's consider people-pleasing.

Have you been a people-pleaser? How has that affected your life? How has your people-pleasing been detrimental?

How can you set boundaries to know when to say yes/no to the time-energy vampires you may have attracted? What mindset do you need to shift to not attract them anymore? Evaluate your beliefs that may have led you to not allowing yourself boundaries?

What have others done for you in the past that you appreciate? Write these down and be sure to write a statement of appreciation. You may even want to send them a note, text, or call them to thank them and share your heartfelt appreciation.

What's going right in your life? No matter how big or small or seemingly insignificant, if you appreciate something that's going right, write it down. Include a statement of appreciation or gratitude. It will feel amazing!

Are you the one demanding someone to please you? If you happen to be the one who is always asking for help, sit with your journal and ask your Inner Being how to view your needs. What can you do to feel better on your own? What beliefs need to shift for you to provide for yourself what you've asked others to do for you? Be sure to appreciate yourself for wanting to align with who you really are!

Chapter 6

Two Ways to Know What's Active in Your Vibration

"The Law of Attraction says what's active in your vibration must continue to increase."
~Abraham-Hicks

Isn't it wonderful when we have a vibration that is increasing the things we want?

What about the times we activate a vibration that increases things we don't want?

How do we know which vibration we have activated?

There are two ways to know what vibration is actively dominant on any subject:

By how we feel.

By what is showing up in our experience.

Let's dissect both of these indicators.

Knowing our active vibration by how we feel:

There are emotions tied to every thought we think. At the

basic level, every thought either feels good or it feels bad. So, there are really only two emotions. It doesn't matter what label you want to put on an emotion – it either feels good or feels bad.

That means we can know without a doubt what kind of thoughts we've been thinking by the way we feel, emotionally. This is the great thing about our emotional guidance system! It works with accuracy for every thought. We don't have to guess about what our thoughts have been – we can simply notice how we're feeling.

If we're feeling good, it indicates that we are in alignment with what our Inner Being is thinking – which is always a nice high vibration attracting more things to feel good about. If we're feeling bad, it's a sure indication that we are not in alignment and thinking in contradiction to what our Inner Being is thinking at the same moment. Bad feelings are always indicating a low vibration which attracts more things to feel bad about. Negative emotions simply mean our contradictory thoughts are indicating resistance.

Whichever way you're feeling is indicating what vibration is active and continuing to increase!

Knowing our active vibration by what is showing up in our experience:

If we notice that good things are primarily coming to us, we can be assured that our dominant vibration is about things we want. We're feeling good. We're appreciative and express our gratitude often. And, that good-feeling indicates that our thoughts are in alignment with our Inner Being's thoughts on the subject we are currently thinking about.

If we notice that unwanted things are primarily coming to us, we can also be assured that our dominant vibration has been about things we don't want or the *lack* of what we do want. We're feeling bad when we look at what's before us. But, we're not feeling bad because of the unwanted stuff coming to us, we were feeling bad long before anything bad-feeling showed up in our experience!

We were originally feeling bad because we were thinking thoughts that felt bad in the first place and those initial thoughts built momentum long enough to attract the unwanted to us!

All vibrations are the instructions or requests we are sending into the Universe. The Universe matches our *active* vibrations and increases them by sending us more experiences that feel like our dominant vibration.

Why does our vibration matter? Why does our vibration increase?

We live in a vibrational Universe. Everything is energy, and as such, energy is creating vibrations. These vibrations are interpreted by the Universe as our request for more. It's not about our thoughts – it's about our emotional vibration. The emotional vibration simply indicates what we have been thinking.

The Universe doesn't understand your words, it understands what you mean or how you're feeling vibrationally. You can be saying all the right words in affirmations, you can be saying things that sound wonderfully inspiring, but the Universe only understands your vibration which may or may not match your words.

You may remember times when you say something nice but on the inside, you feel quite different. Your words and feelings do not match. The vibration of your feelings will always trump your words and be the dominant power in your attraction – by universal law!

Our Inner Being (spirit/soul) has an active vibration on every subject we think about. We, in our mind-body, have an active vibration on every subject, too. So, we contain two vibrational points of attraction. Our job is to align the two points of attraction. Since our Inner Being's point of attraction is always and forever feeling good AND attracting good, it's our mind-body that must be brought back into alignment.

When our mind-body wanders off from feeling good (alignment), then we are in disharmony. Our thoughts are in conflict and hold us apart from who we really are and what we want. **When these two points of attraction are in joyous harmony,**

there is momentum building that catapults us into the receiving mode of the desires we deserve!

Either way, it's always about our thoughts and how they make us feel. This is the vibrational pattern we have going on. This vibrational pattern is our dominant point of attraction.

As we can think thoughts that feel good, we are aligning our active vibration with that of our Inner Being. When alignment happens, there is great power! That is the double-whammy of two powerful points of attraction coming together in harmony. At that moment, you are singular in your power to attract anything you want to be, do or have! That state of cohesiveness is a powerful attractive force.

Do you understand that thoughts create emotions?

Do you understand that emotions attract more thoughts that essentially produce the same feelings?

Do you understand that those thoughts and emotions continue to attract what they are vibrating, building momentum?

And, do you understand that as those emotional vibrations increase to a point they become whatever you're experiencing physically?

Active vibrations must continue to increase – it is law! The Universe's mantra is MORE! We are feeding the Universe more vibrations for It to interpret and add to. There will always be more.

The Universe must expand by Its own law. The Universe's calling for more is what perpetuates eternity. If there was no more asking, it would be game over – and that can never happen!

How do you shift your active vibration to increase more of what you do want?

There are two really good ways to activate a higher vibration that attracts more of what you want. These are great ways to bring that cohesiveness to our spirit-mind-body into pure alignment for powerfully focused energy.

Meditate and quiet your mind daily for 15-20 minutes. This is a thought-focusing practice that will help when you need to focus your thoughts at other times of the day. When you quiet your thoughts, you also quiet resistant thoughts which naturally raises your vibration. It also aligns you with your Inner Being when you quiet your mind long enough to hear inspiration, new thoughts, and impulses to act.

Practice segment intending. Stop and consciously set intentions for how you want to feel and what you want to experience in each segment of your day. (A segment is every time your situation changes – getting up in the morning, driving to work, moving through your work-day, making a call, someone entering your space, etc.)

Both of these practices are excellent ways to energetically get out ahead of what's coming next. It's preparing your energetic environment so you'll be more receptive to what you truly want to experience and receive.

It's really fun to set your intention for a segment and then look back at what you created! The more you practice this, the better you'll get at creating a joy-filled life one segment at a time!

Deliberately doing practices that raise our vibration is the key to experiencing more joy!

The main point of shifting your vibrational output is to get out ahead of the vibration, energetically, for the purpose of feeling better. Feeling better is always the goal. Feeling good should be your number one priority. You must learn to be selfish enough to care about how you feel if you ever want to allow good things to flow into your experience.

Remember, we came here to experience as much joy as possible. If you are not in joy more and more of the time, you are missing out on your best life!

Since feeling good is the goal, when you reach that place of feeling really good, revel in the feeling. Take time to savor the feeling. Allow it to gain momentum and become your dominant vibrational expression. Don't try to make something happen or solve a problem, just yet. Allow the good feeling to stabilize. This good-feeling is where your power resides!

This good-feeling will be your new active vibration and begin to increase. This newly expanded vibration will send out waves of instructions into the Universe. As it grows in momentum and power, the Universe must yield to you more things that match its vibrational quality - which is the wonderful stuff you've already put into your energetic vortex of creation.

The better you feel, the better you'll feel. This is the sweet spot of living authentically who we are as joy in these amazing physical bodies!

Integrative Exercises

Use the following writing prompts this week to help you integrate what you've learned for your transformation.

These two practices should become part of your daily routine. I know these have been repeated because they are foundational to your alignment. If you would add these two, alone, you would be an aligned powerhouse!

Meditate daily for 15-20 minutes. I like to use a meditation app like InsightTimer because I can find ambient sounds that coincide with their timer. To keep my mind quiet, I choose an ambient sound to focus on that is a bit slower. Some of their ambient sound choices are a bit too stimulating for me. You'll have to find one that resonates with you.

Or, you can simply listen for the sound of the air conditioning system, the whirring of a ceiling fan, a dripping faucet, the chirping of birds, or the wind in the trees. Any sound that is not too interesting that doesn't stimulate thought. Counting your slow deep breaths helps to quiet your mind.

Practice holding the thought of the sound in your mind and allow any other thoughts to come up and be released. Always returning to the sound. You will eventually feel a detachment in your body. You may experience visions, colors, or smells. You may get sensations in your body.

When the timer goes off, take a deep cleansing breath, wiggle your fingers and toes, and gently open your eyes.

You could even begin a meditation journal. Write about your meditation experiences. How did you feel? Did you see anything in your mind's eye? Did you smell something? Were you with anyone? Did you receive messages, ideas, inspiration to do something? Did you receive a gut knowing about a decision you need to make?

Maybe you love to dance and move your body after meditation to embody the feeling of love and joy you experienced. Or, maybe you feel really creative and want to write something, a poem, book, or story. Creating any kind of art is an expression of love and joy - who you really are.

Practice Intention Setting throughout your day. When we mindfully move through each segment of our day, we are energetically projecting our desired vibration out ahead of us. Before you change segments, stop and ask yourself:

How do I want to feel? *(Think of emotional words and states of being that feel really good.)*

What do I want to experience? *(Things that are beneficial for all involved.)*

It only takes seconds to practice segment-intending but the rewards are amazing. It's even fun to write down your segment intentions in a journal or notebook and look back on the day to see what you created! Seeing your progress really encourages you to keep doing it. Make it fun!

Chapter 7

Thieves of Joy

When you're just not feeling joyful, what do you do?

Do you look around for someone or something to blame? As if some outside force stole your joy?

Or, do you begin to look inward to see if your thoughts and limiting beliefs might be the culprit?

What are your thieves of joy? Do any of these sound familiar?

- Complaining.
- Comparing.
- Judging.
- Believing the lies of indoctrinated beliefs.
- Resentment.
- Unworthiness.
- Competing.
- People-pleasing.
- Not speaking your truth.
- Believing everything you think.

There are a host of thieves that will come in to steal our joy when we're not paying attention. Maybe you're beginning to recognize the thieves more quickly now that you've been on your transformational journey for a while. Maybe you've become more aware of how you feel earlier in the game and can find thoughts that soothe your emotions.

Maybe you no longer beat yourself up for having negative feelings and allow yourself to feel all the feels at that moment. And, then, you're ready to say, *Okay, that's enough of that and I'm ready to feel better now and move forward.*

What are the triggers that you notice when you realize your joy is waning or maybe gone?

When I become aware that I'm heading into a shitty mood, I have all the tools that could help but I don't always use them. *Ugh! Why do I do this? I've been on my transformational journey and studying the law of attraction for years. I know this stuff and I teach this stuff!*

Now, I do want to acknowledge that I'm doing way better than I did years ago but I'd also like to get even better at this transition back into my joy, faster and more efficiently. When my mind goes spinning out of control and I *allow* my thoughts to run unchecked, I sink very quickly into complaining and resentment. I was thoroughly trained and raised to be a people-pleaser without regard to speaking my truth! So, I kinda understand how I get myself out of whack sometimes. I'm still learning to be gentle with myself.

I've been trained so well that it's not good to rock the boat.

And, speaking up for myself, speaking my truth about my desires could evoke an unwanted response from the other(s). My fear of speaking up has clearly held me in the prison of playing small in life and my business. And, at times, eating me up on the inside!

I know my triggers are becoming resentful, complaining, and angry, usually at someone because they hurt my feelings or didn't do something we talked about. Or, it could be I simply *expected* them to read my mind and KNOW that I wanted this thing or for them to do something for me! This usually shows up because I've not given myself permission to ask for what I want, need, or simply desire. And, then, I get angry at myself because I can't bring myself to speak up for myself and I resent the other person for not just *knowing* what I want! *Uh, duh!*

So, then, I go into beating myself up for *still* not being able to speak up for myself. *I'm 62 for crying out loud! Why am I still doing this?* I also know that I still am struggling with my need to control situations and people. I find myself blowing up when I finally have had enough of not getting what I want and spewing it out there AT the other person, instead of not allowing it to get so explosive in me before I speak up. When I blow a gasket, for some reason they tend to react and don't receive it well, either. *Imagine that!*

Since I'm out of alignment at that moment and not speaking from a place of love for myself or them, it never turns out well. My energy is ugly and that's what I receive back from the person I'm almost attacking.

Happily, this is happening less and less as I'm working on healing my toxic indoctrinated beliefs that I learned from a childhood raised in a very evangelical, patriarchal type church and family. Instead of holding in all my desires, I'm finally able to ask for things more frequently. I'm living a much more satisfying and peaceful life! I'm still a work in progress, though, to be sure!!

What have I learned about the thieves of joy stealing from us?

I've come to understand this about our attraction – good or bad, wanted or unwanted. It's all about momentum. When we have too much momentum going in a negative direction because we haven't been deliberately choosing our thoughts, the Universe simply obeys its law and matches what we have going on vibrationally. Of course, this works either way - positive and negative.

So, this law of attraction will certainly work in our favor IF we can nip our negative thoughts in the bud. But, we have to be aware we're in this pattern of thought early enough before the momentum builds too much. Then, deliberately shift our thoughts to those that feel better - even a little better!

Momentum matters because once we are gaining momentum in our thought-vibration, we can't stop on a dime and head in the opposite direction. We can't be in joy and suddenly shift gears and react to something with anger. Nor can we be in anger and suddenly experience joy a second later. These energies are on opposite ends of the vibrational frequencies spectrum.

We can, however, be in joy - really feeling good and in alignment - and as the peak of our joy wanes and slows down, we don't reinforce our joy by looking for something else to appreciate and enjoy to keep the momentum going. Instead, we may hear something or see something we don't like and allow ourselves to give it some attention. We feel the twinge of an emotion attached to our thoughts about not wanting that thing we've noticed. But, did we actually pay attention that we felt that twinge of negative emotion creeping in?

That twinge of not feeling good was our warning bell – thieves of joy are circling our perimeter!

If we've ignored the initial signal, then we think a little more about that thing we don't want. The more we stay in that pattern of thought the Universe is obediently matching us with more thoughts that feel the same. Now, our thoughts are gaining momentum! We run into someone who mentions the thing we don't want and now we are co-creating even more momentum in that direction until it's full steam ahead!

We feel disappointed or angry. The complaining kicks in. We judge this thing as bad or wrong. *Sirens blaring!* We have just been robbed! We just allowed our thieves of joy to rob us!

Fortunately, this momentum can work in our favor, too.

So, how can we become more aware of what we are thinking?

That's where we have a secret weapon against the thieves of our joy!

Our secret weapon against our thieves of joy is our inner emotional guidance! As you know by now, our emotions tell on our thoughts every single time. Think about it. Every time we think a thought, we have an emotional response. When we feel bad, we have been thinking negative thoughts. When we feel good, we have been thinking positive thoughts.

Test it out. The next time you feel crappy, stop a minute and recall what your previous thoughts were. Or, the next time you're feeling good, evaluate what your thoughts were immediately before you felt good. It's an easy test and works every time!

We have this amazingly helpful tool of our emotions that will serve us well IF we put it to use for our advantage. It's way too difficult to control the 60,000 to 80,000 thoughts we have in a day. *That ain't happening!* The cool thing is that each of those thoughts has an emotional response attached to them.

So, it's *way easier* to notice how we feel and decide what we're going to do from there. It's a whole lot easier to notice that we're feeling bad and realize we have been on a rampage of negative thoughts. That negative emotion is simply indicating that we have been thinking thoughts that are contradictory or in opposition to what our Inner Being is thinking at the very same time about the very same subject!

Our emotions indicate the direction we're heading. They are our security system!

When we feel good, we are heading in the direction of more of what we want and our Inner Being is saying, *YES! That's it – warmer, warmer!* Feeling good is the green light to proceed happily and securely.

When we feel bad, we are heading in the direction of more of what we don't want or we are holding ourselves in the position of the lack or absence of what we do want. During those crappy-feeling times, our Inner Being is saying, *Dude! I just see it way different and the outcome is outrageously awesome! Colder, colder. Think like me!* Feeling bad is the red flashing warning light that joy thieves are on the premises!

How do we maintain the security of our joy?

We keep our connection lines open with our Inner Being and monitor our security system - our emotions - frequently!

When we become more aware of how we feel at every moment, we are tuned into our security system. When it gives us early warning signs with the first negative emotion, HALT and do not proceed any further. Say, *OMG! I'm doing that thing again and it's totally an unnecessary thought.* Then, laugh and pat yourself on the back and say, *Good job ME! I was awake and aware!*

This is when we have the ability to use our emotions to guide us back into a feeling-better attitude. It's our attitude, our mood, in every moment that allows or disallows our flow of joy! **The thoughts we choose to focus on will continue to build our momentum toward more joy or move away from our joy.**

So, it's time to make feeling good our number one priority. It's time to be so selfish about feeling good that *nothing* can ever stop us from *choosing joy* whenever we want to improve our attitude and outcome. Our choice of thoughts is under our control. Let's learn to use our control wisely.

Let's be so devoted to ourselves that we choose joy more and more of the time. Let's be so loyal and loving toward ourselves that we can speak our truth with love. Let's be so enthusiastic about the joys of life that we focus on more things that we appreciate! *Now, there's some powerful alignment!*

When we are in joy, enjoying life, we have become whole. We are one with who we really are as extensions of Source Energy. We are one with our Inner Source. We are knowing, thinking, and feeling exactly the same way as our Inner Source – the Source of All Joy!

Then, no real harm can ever befall us. We will attract more

things that expand the joy we already feel. When we do see something we don't want, we will understand it's simply our opportunity to ask for our personal improvement on the subject. If we choose to think more like our Inner Being, we will feel joy expand exponentially! It must. It's law! And, no thieves can approach us to steal our joy!

Integrative Exercises

Use the following writing prompts this week to help you integrate what you've learned for your transformation.

What are the thieves of your joy? What are the triggers that get activated and knock you out of alignment with your joy? Triggers can be activated from past trauma or indoctrinated limiting beliefs. Refer back to the list at the beginning of this lesson. Do any of those resonate with you? Write about why they are triggers. What can you shift in your thoughts to bring you relief? If they make you feel bad, you may want to dance it out, beat a drum, or do whatever would move the energy up and out of your body to release the emotions.

Practice noticing how you are feeling throughout the day. To get in the habit of this, set alarms on your phone hourly or every couple of hours. When the alarm goes off, quickly assess how you're feeling emotionally. Reflect on your previous thoughts and adjust them as necessary to feel better. If you can get your thoughts back up to joy and appreciation, you're the champ of the bonus round! Truly, any feeling of relief or feeling better is kudos to you! If you can feel a little better now, you can always feel even better with some more practice.

How will you make feeling good your number one priority? What will you need to shift to allow yourself to feel more joyful? Write about what you will do to support you in noticing how you feel and making joy your priority. Anything that reminds you to feel into your joy throughout the day.

Chapter 8

How to Move Into Joy When You're Just Not Feeling It

We all want to feel joyful! *Heck, I'd just be happy to feel a little relief by feeling hopeful!* Okay, so you know you, at least, want to feel better. Maybe joyful is too much of a stretch for you right now. But, deep down inside, you *know* being joyful would be your dream emotion.

Do you know why?

We all want to feel joyful because it is who we really are!

Our Inner Beings ARE joyful. And, since we are an extension in the physical, of that joy, we are all being called to live in that joy. Our Inner Beings are always feeling good and calling us to feel good, too.

> *"You are joy, looking for a way to express. It's not just that your purpose is joy, it is that you are joy. You are love and joy and freedom and clarity expressing. Energy – frolicking and eager – that's who you are. And so, if you're always reaching for alignment with that, you're always on your path, and your path will take you into all kinds of places. You are Pure Positive Energy that translates into the human emotion of joy."* ~Abraham-Hicks

Remember this quote from the first lesson? I had to repeat it here because this quote sends shivers of delight all over me! But, it wasn't always that way! There were many years that I couldn't even think about being joyful - it wasn't even on my radar.

I complained and kicked and bucked at everything. I held a victim mentality that only brought more victimization into my experience. I played a really good martyr!

One of my jokingly favorite sayings was *Poor, poor Mary Ann.* And, I'd pooch my bottom lip out to show how poorly I was treated in life. All kidding aside, I really *felt* that way on the inside even though it became my signature joke within my family. I was severely depressed at different times during my life – on the verge of taking my life.

My Inner Being was calling me to joy even through my resistance.

Thankfully, my Inner Being was still calling me because I didn't really want to be done with this life. What I was really looking for was a release of my resistance. I wanted the pain to end – not my life! I appreciate that I made it through those times. They did pass and eventually, my asking was answered!

My path started lighting up as I began giving up my resistant thoughts. I evaluated my indoctrinated beliefs and discarded many of them. In their place, I decided what beliefs really resonated with my soul. Things in my life began shifting when I gave up being angry about everything and toward everyone.

The more I practiced looking for positive things that were going right in my life, the better I felt. I stopped resisting my natural well-being that was waiting for me to allow it to flow through me! I didn't understand this in the beginning but the more I felt better – emotionally, physically, and spiritually – I knew I was on the right track!

I became a bit more eager and hopeful that help was on the way. I hired coaches and mentors and invested in programs to guide me closer to my goal of dynamic thriving! I've come to understand that every single person on a quest needs a guide!

Of course, this transformation didn't come overnight. It was many years in the making. I'm so grateful that I kept looking for ways to live a better life. I was beginning to hear the calling of my Inner Being from this new perspective.

I made the decision that I wanted to feel better, so I started *looking* for better-feeling thoughts and beliefs. I learned that beliefs were simply thoughts I kept repeating to myself until I believed them. I realized that would be the way I could improve my life – by repeating thoughts that felt better to me so I would begin to believe them, instead! I allowed those resistant thoughts and beliefs to fade away by focusing my attention on thoughts and beliefs that resonated with my soul–which felt pretty darned good!!

You may be saying,

Yeah, blah, blah, blah! How am I supposed to be joyful when I'm not anywhere close to feeling it?!

If you're like me, you truly want to get up in the morning and absolutely love your life! But, when we're not feeling it, it can be difficult to imagine a life that feels good – much less joyful!

So often, we simply are not in a place of joy. We are on lower levels of the emotional scale. We may be in fear, doubt, misery, anger, depression, or even utter dis-empowerment like I used to be. We want to be in joy but we're just not even close to that emotional level.

Rest assured that all is well! You can't make that quantum leap from despair into joy in one swoop! You wouldn't want to. If you've been feeling bad for a while, you have a lot of momentum going in that direction. So, be easy with yourself. You can learn to take baby steps up the emotional scale, step-by-step into better feeling emotions.

Here is the list of emotions that are presented by Abraham-Hicks, my mentor, in their book, *Ask and It Is Given*:

1. Joy/Knowledge/Empowerment/Freedom/Love/Appreciation

2. Passion
3. Enthusiasm/Eagerness/Happiness
4. Positive Expectation/Belief
5. Optimism
6. Hopefulness
7. Contentment
8. Boredom
9. Pessimism
10. Frustration/Irritation/Impatience
11. "Overwhelment"
12. Disappointment
13. Doubt
14. Worry
15. Blame
16. Discouragement
17. Anger
18. Revenge
19. Hatred/Rage
20. Jealousy
21. Insecurity/Guilt/Unworthiness
22. Fear/Grief/Depression/Despair/Powerlessness

Simply reading through this list, you can feel the emotional vibrational variation of each word. **When we read words that express an emotional response, we can viscerally feel them in our bodies. You felt it didn't you?** As you began reading the list, you felt better at the top than when you reached the bottom of the list, didn't you? That's how powerful these emotions are.

As you can see there are many steps in between Fear/Grief/Depression/Despair/Powerlessness and Joy/Knowledge/Empowerment/Freedom/Love/Appreciation! You simply cannot make that quantum leap from 22 to 1! It just doesn't work that way. It's an impossible emotional leap but it would also be too hard on your body, energetically.

The Law of Attraction won't let you make that kind of quantum leap, energetically or vibrationally. You may have had too much momentum going on where you are to make that kind of leap to a totally different emotional vibration. And, that's as it should be. You must ease into each next higher level of emotion, gently.

Negative emotions are not a bad thing! Our emotions are given to us as an indicator of where our thoughts have been focused – toward what we do want or what we don't want. Every thought either feels good or bad. Period.

I know I'm about to repeat myself but I know I'm a forgetful person and maybe you are too. So, here goes…our emotions tell on our thoughts every single time, so noticing how you feel is the best way to determine what direction your thoughts have been heading.

So, all emotions are simply indicating where you are,

energetically, right here, right now. Do you want to know where you are at any given moment? Feeling bad is simply indicating you are focused more on what you don't want and heading in that direction. When you catch a glimpse of feeling good, it is indicating that you are currently heading in the direction of what you do want.

So, here's what you can do to move up the emotional scale into a more joy-filled life experience step-by-step.

When you find yourself feeling less than joyful, don't beat up on yourself for not feeling joyful. Be kind to yourself, first! Then find the best-feeling emotion you can reach for at that moment from where you are.

Empower yourself by saying, *I can't get all the way to joy but I can choose a better-feeling emotion from where I am now.* If you are in despair you can probably find a better-feeling thought of anger. Yes, anger can be a better-feeling thought! Who knew?!

Pat yourself on the back because you *deliberately* chose a different thought! Then, consciously recognize that you found relief in that slightly better-feeling thought. **If you can feel a little better now, you can feel a little better again!**

Acknowledge that you did feel better going from despair to anger. You may upset a lot of people when you reach anger from despair because they liked you better and could handle you better when you were in despair! Don't let them deter you and don't hang out in anger very long either before reaching for more relief!

Once you feel some better in anger, then reach for disappointment or even up to irritation. Know that you live in an environment that is perfect because you do have the freedom to choose – that's free will. Freedom is the basis of your life! It's really the basis that all life is built upon and so important to all of us!

Begin noticing that the Universe responds readily to what you're giving your attention to. As your vibration shifts into a higher emotional vibration, the Universe will respond in kind and match your new vibration with those better-feeling thoughts or experiences.

Notice what's manifesting in your life as a result of your deliberate shift in feelings. Manifestations indicate in what direction you are heading. The better you start feeling, the better-feeling manifestations will be attracted to you!

Remember that your Inner Being is always feeling good and in love with your life. Your Inner Being is calling YOU to be in love with your life, too! That's why you want to feel more joyful – it's at the core of who you really are!

Make it your dominant intention to always reach for thoughts that bring emotional relief. If you're unwilling to make it your intention to feel good, you're going to end up wallowing in the same old low vibrational thoughts which continue to create the same old life just with different faces, different places. Or, you can be willing to do the work of reaching for better-feeling thoughts and creating something new. It's your choice! That's how free you truly are!

Many times we want to see our lives change and improve but we're not willing to do the vibrational, energetic work. We have to be willing to deliberately choose better-feeling thoughts for our lives to manifest better-feeling conditions.

"Thinking is the hardest work there is, which is probably the reason why so few engage in it."
~Henry Ford

Yikes! Ouch! I'm inclined to agree with Mr. Ford here. We want to see an improvement in our lives but too many times we're not willing to do the inner work. Our inner work is to take control of our thoughts, put on our big girl panties and choose our thoughts by how they make us feel! Let's use our determination to engage in thinking by how it makes us feel!! That will attract the change we so desire.

I had to do this work–heck, I'm still doing this work! It's a life-long process because we will never get it done as eternal beings. It never stops. We never stop Being.

Every day I have to make the decision moment-by-moment to choose how I want to feel and pick my thoughts deliberately. When I feel myself heading down the slippery slope of negativity, it's time to reign in my thoughts before they make off with my emotional wagon like a team of wild horses. When my thoughts give me a subtle nudge of negativity, I need to actively jump on the wagon and take control by re-focusing my thoughts toward what feels better.

As you make strides in moving up the emotional scale, gently, you can continue working your way up to joy! It will only take as long to navigate up the emotional scale as you are willing to do the work. To evaluate where you are, look at the levels of improved emotions and choose the next better-feeling vibration. It will get quite exciting when you feel your progress moving up the scale!

All of life is about NOW!

No matter what is going on with your circumstances, all of life is about your life experience NOW. It's about the feeling-journey while your circumstances have time to begin shifting. It's not about making or forcing the circumstances to change, which leads you into a false sense of control. It's about how you think and feel about your NOW, which is solely under your control.

Begin shifting your emotional vibration and give the Universe time to respond. You will eventually see new manifestations soon enough. The Universe is all set up to respond to your vibration NOW - not a few minutes ago or not even in a few minutes from now - but NOW!

Every NOW is constantly shifting into a new NOW. So, it's important to be mindful of how you are feeling at every moment in time. Remember, those feelings are telling on your thoughts every single time! *This is one time that tattle-tailing is beneficial! Ha!*

Begin feeling your way up the emotional scale to your heart's desire. As you incrementally move up the emotional scale you'll feel better and the Universe will yield to you your heart's desire! Everything you want is possible. We live in a Universe of unlimited possibilities!

You can feel when your thoughts bring relief or create more stressful pressure. Right? You can feel more or less stressed according to the thoughts you are choosing. And, the best part of all is that you have complete freedom to choose your own thoughts! No one else can think one thought for you. No one can be on your emotional scale with you. Only you get to choose!

Now, you can let others influence your thoughts, but that again is your choice. You cannot be forced to think like anyone else! If you're allowing others to influence your thoughts, you are pinching yourself off from the thoughts that your Inner Being is thinking. You are not under the influence of your own Inner Being. You are allowing others to be your influencer – and that's never a beneficial place to be!

Don't ever feel that you must justify to others or even yourself why you are in the place you are. That will be of no benefit – and even do more harm by dragging you down further. Don't listen to anyone - even yourself - who is accusing you of being stuck in a bad place. You're not bad, you've just been creating your reality by default – unconsciously.

Stop saying you're bad or unworthy. Start telling the story of your life as you want it to be. *I am good! I am worthy! I am joyful! I truly AM GOOD and I'm going to start living as if I truly believe it!*

Begin making conscious decisions about your thoughts because you want to feel better. Make it your dominant intent to choose your thoughts by how they feel. When you reach for a thought that feels better, pat yourself on the back, and revel in your newfound power!!

You innately know that all good things should come to good people. Your Inner Being is knowing, thinking, and feeling that you ARE a good person. That's why your inner scream is that you want good things because you ARE a good person at the core of who you really are! *(Hint: If you ever get any message that is critical or degrading of you in any way, it's NOT from your Inner Being.)*

You should never have to suffer in any way. You are really, really good, and good stuff should be manifesting in your life. The only reason any of us suffer is because of our own resistance! We are pinching ourselves off from the influence of our Inner Being. We are listening to and believing what others have taught us or told us instead of what our Inner Being knows, thinks, and feels about us. Which is, that we are totally awesome!!

That's why we want to feel joyful so intensely. It's our Inner Being calling us to be who we really are - JOY! And, we really want to BE who we really are!

Realizing that contrast is showing you the difference in what you don't want versus what you do want is the starting place. You have to know the difference between them by how you feel. That's the perfect gauging system. What better way to know what you do want than by seeing what you don't want? You must have something to compare. Feeling good is what you want. Feeling bad is what you don't want. You create your life experience by how you feel.

You came here to create! Create the life of your dreams. To feel as much joy as possible. You came here to focus your thought-energy toward things you want. And, you know that when you have these things you will feel better – that's why we want anything–to feel better. But, you also knew that you must feel good, first, before your creation can manifest! It's joyful to create. And, you create happily-ever-after by choosing joy!

It's always about the fun trek along the way. It's about feeling good. It's about being eager for more. It's about knowing that you can't get it wrong because you can never get it done – as an eternal being. It's never really about the destination – it's about the experiential journey along the way!

It's about BEING more than DOING or HAVING. Yes, we adore doing and having but it's mostly about being – the enjoyment of the journey. It's about molding your own energy. It's about the connection with who you really are! And, who you really are is JOY!

Integrative Exercises

Use the following writing prompts this week to help you integrate what you've learned for your transformation.

Notice how you're feeling right now. Do you feel not very good, pretty good, or great? Just notice how you're feeling at the moment and find the emotional word that corresponds to how you're feeling on the emotional scale list above.

Unless you're at number 1, you could do some energy work to move up closer to that number 1 of joy, right? Granted, numbers 1-5 are pretty awesome! Once you determine where you are on the emotional scale, decide where you'd like to be. Write some thoughts that would feel better and help you move up one step at a time. Write as many as you need to get you up a few more levels. Where did you begin and where did you end during this session?

Again, you may want to express each upward level by dance, moving your body to music, art, or anything creative that feels like the emotional levels as you're moving up through the scale.

Do this exercise daily over the next week. Or, do it quickly every time you notice how you're feeling each day. Set alarms on your phone throughout the day to help you remember to stop and notice how you're feeling. This helps you get in the habit of noticing your emotions which will indicate the direction you are heading - toward wanted or unwanted experiences.

Always, always, always end on a positive thought pattern to raise your vibration. If you're feeling better, you know you'll have accomplished your goal of making feeling better your priority!

Chapter 9

Know Who You Really Are

Love yourself first, so you know who you really are!

How do you talk to yourself? Are you critical and resistant to praising and loving yourself?

When you look in the mirror do you see someone you love or someone you disdain?

How have those conversations with yourself made you feel? Do you feel uplifted or down in the dumps, maybe to the point of depression at times?

Since I know, personally, what it's like to get so disgusted with the person I see in the mirror, I'm talking to myself throughout this lesson, too. I've had the same conversations that you've probably had with yourself – being critical, ashamed, guilty, ugly, fat, stupid, out of control, just too much, too sensitive, and the like.

It's time to change those kinds of conversations with ourselves. I know I feel a tugging to change my attitude about myself because that's not the life I want to live. It's certainly not the life we intended for ourselves when we were non-physical and desiring to come into the physical as the person we are in this time-space reality. I know deep down within me, those critical words are *not* who I really am. They stem from indoctrinated beliefs that I *learned* to believe.

I want to live a happy, carefree life full of joy and love for myself! I can't get there by being critical during my self-talk.

I want to see my experiences improve. I want so many things that I've always held myself back from, because of my small, dis-empowered mindset.

I want to be that beautiful pure, positive light that I know I am!

The only reason we ever want something in this life is that we believe we will feel better by having it. And that's a good thing! That desire means we are living and breathing eternal creators. We are expanding every day. We are never the same person two days in a row!

The whole point of this life is to live in joy, happiness and have fun creating new things.

Let's see what we can do to improve our self-talk....

1. Tell a new story. Just because we observe things in our lives and our attitudes about ourselves, doesn't mean we have to stay that way. It's time to tell a new story about how we want our lives to be—who we want to be. It's time to NOT face reality – it's time to

CREATE reality. And, the only way we can do that is to deliberately distract our thoughts from what we observe as reality - which is always temporary - and focus our thoughts on what we want our lives to be.

The more you reinforce bad thoughts about yourself, the more you will find evidence and proof to believe that's who you are. You say that's reality. But that's just creating from your past dominant thoughts and it's time to create a new story about you – by thinking better thoughts and remembering who you really are.

2. Believe *before* seeing. The true path to getting real change in your life is believing *before* you see the manifestation in physical form. We tend to think that we will believe it *after* we see our circumstances change, but that is backward. Faith comes before seeing the physical manifestation or better circumstances. You must believe first.

Once you've sent a desire into your vortex (the place where all vibrational energy of your desires are held) it is answered immediately by Source Energy. You have to realize that your desires exist in a vibrational reality even *before* you can see them!

3. Stop beating yourself up because you're not seeing any results yet. You have to feel that it exists and, then, take joy in knowing your answer is on the way – calling you to it. Your work is to simply get into alignment with your desires by feeling good and you will vibrate at the same frequency of your desires; drawing them into your physical reality.

It is always, always, always a *feeling* process – not a *doing* process. It is not action-based, it is feeling-based. The action comes later with inspiration. Appreciate yourself for taking the time to practice feeling good. And, your very first manifestation of something you desire coming is indicated by feeling good!

4. Go general with your thoughts to feel your way into alignment with your desires. When we desire something strongly, we sometimes get caught up in the details of it. By focusing on the details, we notice the contrast between the having of it and the *lack* of having it. We tend to start noticing the lack of having it. That activates even more energy of not having it in our experience – it slows down the process of receiving.

So, it's best to go general with your thoughts and that simply means, don't put in so many details, yet. Think about how it will *feel* when you do receive your desire. Think in terms of wonderful emotionally descriptive words or good-feeling states of being. We'll talk more about how to do this in the Integrative Exercises.

When we slow down the process by noticing that what we want isn't here, yet, this is when we tend to start beating ourselves up with our self-talk. So, to soothe your bad feelings of lack you must go general and distract yourself from noticing the lack. You want to notice things that make you feel really good! That's why making lists of favorite things is so important – things that you love, lists of positive aspects of your life, things you appreciate, and really make you happy when you think about them.

5. Think about anything or any subject that feels really good when you think about it. This will allow you to vibrate at the highest level and match what's in your vortex and by universal law, it must start showing up in your reality. Yes, it takes tons of practice, but you will be rewarded with feeling good and you will see the shift in your mindset and experience. When you feel good you more easily speak in a kind and loving way to yourself!

6. Every day, look in the mirror and make loving statements to yourself. Now that you've been practicing better-feeling thoughts, you are ready to start applying them to your self-talk. You've been writing lists of wonderfully delicious things that you appreciate. It's time to insert yourself into the equation. Talk to yourself like you're praising or complimenting or telling someone just how much you love them and why. You may not believe everything you say to yourself in the mirror at first, but in time, you will start to fall in love with YOU!

7. Be gentle with yourself. It's really okay not to figure it all out at once. Allow yourself as long a learning curve as necessary, because you'll never get it done and you'll never get it wrong. Creation is eternal and always expanding. It can never retreat or go backward. Your path is unfolding at the right time and in the right ways. Be as gentle and tender with your feelings as this will keep you feeling good. Appreciate your gentle spirit!

8. Make your opinion of yourself and feeling good more important than any other person's opinion of you. Matter of fact, make feeling good your highest priority! Yes, that's selfishness in its purest form. If you don't make feeling good your top priority – no one else will – it's not their job!

We're not talking about an egotistical kind of selfishness. We are talking about real unconditional love–basing your love and care for yourself not upon conditions, but on pure compassion. Can you imagine what a beautiful world we would have if everyone kept their love for feeling good at the heart of every decision?

When you focus on feeling good, you are aligned with Source and you can never make a decision that will hurt anyone or anything while aligned with Source! The Source within you is calling you to your highest expression of love.

You are Source. You are love. You are perfection. You are joy! This should be your opinion of yourself – because it IS Source's opinion of YOU! Appreciate your growing fondness for yourself.

With this process, you will be able to have loving conversations with yourself. You will be able to see things that you appreciate about yourself.

Once you get in alignment with the Source within you, you will get urges to do something or go somewhere or talk with someone. These are rendezvous with cooperative components to help create the life you love. Take time to appreciate that you are hearing from your Inner Source's guidance.

Tell yourself how much you appreciate yourself, for being still and listening. As you do take inspired actions, really enjoy yourself. Be excited and expect good things to come into your awareness and reality. Tell yourself how excited you are! Feel your excitement!

Watch for *winks* from the universe that all is well and notice the rendezvous the Universe has set up for you. Tell yourself how much fun you're having watching all the synchronicity and coincidence of the Universe working on your behalf. Remind yourself that Source has your back.

Tell your body how much you appreciate her for carrying you around in this life and serving you well. Appreciate that each cell knows exactly what they need to do to keep you healthy. With trillions of cells working on your behalf you have a lot to be thankful for - so express your gratitude to you!

Most of all, remembering who you really are will go a long way in having loving conversations with yourself.

Affirm today: *I am pure, positive energy. I am the creator of my reality. I am an extension of Source Energy. I am love. I am perfect. I am worthy. I am expanding and growing every day. I am joy! All is well!*

Integrative Exercises

Use the following writing prompts this week to help you integrate what you've learned for your transformation.

Do you know who you really are? You can determine that answer by your evaluating your self-talk! When you speak to yourself, is it loving and joyfully appreciative? Or, is it critical and judgmental? When you can begin to speak to yourself in loving, appreciative ways, then you can truly say you *know* who you really are. Your Inner Being never lies about your goodness and joy!

So, what has your self-talk been like? Write down some of the phrases you tell yourself as you move through your day. Ask close friends or family, *What do I say about myself? How have you heard me talk about myself or describe myself?* Write down what they say and consider if those phrases or descriptions need to change to a more loving, appreciative description.

How would you like it to improve? How would you talk to a loved one if they were in the same position in which you find yourself? Would you be loving and patient or would you be critical and judgmental in your conversation with them? Write down some of the phrases you know you've heard yourself say to someone you love - especially, how you comfort them when they're feeling low. Now, say these to YOU!

If you *knew* that you were joy embodied, unconditionally

loving, and pure positive light and love, how would you speak to yourself? Write what that conversation would be if you really *believed* this was who you really are. Better yet, tell yourself how wonderful you really are by recording your voice on your voice recording app on your phone. Listen back to all the goodness of you!

Write affirmations that you can begin speaking to yourself. It is especially beneficial to say these statements as you look at yourself in the mirror. You will come to believe them as you repeat them to yourself - beliefs are only thoughts you repeat to yourself until they become your belief - your truth. Create a new truth if you need to!

Here are a few you could begin with and build your own from this beginning place:

I am pure, positive energy. I am the creator of my reality. I am an extension of Source Energy. I am love. I am perfect. I am worthy. I am expanding and growing every day. I am joy! All is well!

Go general with your thoughts! When we get too specific with our thoughts around our desires, they can turn into noticing we don't have those things, yet. Then, we've split our energy and we hold what we want away from us. But, if we can think in more general *feeling* terms, we hold longer to the feelings that raise our vibration because we're focusing on the general good feelings. We do not have to get specific until we are stable in a good-feeling place.

So, here's what that looks like: You want to focus on wonderful-feeling expressions of emotional words that you're feeling or positive states of being. *(Examples: I want to feel good. Feeling good feels like happiness, joy, peace, abundance, choices, confidence, adventure, safety, excitement, exhilaration, support, clarity, hope, well-being, security, etc.)* Feel into every word or state of being as you write! The more time you spend feeling like this, the Universe will inspire you to write even more or even repeat words that really resonate with your soul! Have fun with this. Dance, sing, laugh, paint, hug a tree!

Chapter 10

Have a Great Day
(Unless You've Made Other Plans)

"Have a great day!"

How many times have you been wished a great day in passing?

Maybe, someone you love wished you a great day, so you knew they really meant it.

Did you take them up on it?

Did you *decide* to have a great day? Or, did you make other plans?

How much planning goes into having a great day?

For starters, your great day begins the night before. A great day is something you *intend* and plan for. A great day cannot be left to chance. There is some effort in creating great days!

If you're in a crappy mood when you go to sleep, you'll most likely wake up in the same crappy mood. This isn't rocket science. If there's momentum going, it will be more difficult to stop it and turn things around.

It doesn't have to be that way, because when you sleep your momentum from the previous day's thoughts subside. This is really good to know! As your previous day's thoughts subside during sleep, this includes your resistant thoughts.

When you awaken, you have a fresh day to start anew. You are blessed with a brand new baby day! Only *you* choose what kind of day you will experience.

You could wake up and start thinking about where you left off the night before, and that could be either good or bad, happy or crappy, empowered or disempowered. It's always your choice for the kind of day you'll have.

If you'd like to plan on having a great day, start the night before and when you lay your head on that pillow, think of things you appreciate.

Appreciate the roof over your head, the conditioned air, the cozy bed and blankies, your fluffy pillow.

Appreciate the well-being you experience – even if you're sick or hurting, there are still functions of your body that are operating properly without your direct management required! *This was really big for me as I was moving out of being such a sick person and learning to appreciate my body's well-being. I chose to list all the parts and functions I could think of that were working right and appreciate them. And, sort of ignore the parts that were sick or hurting! It helped so much, I still continue to appreciate my body in this way! I even thank my body for performing functions I don't even know about or understand!*

Appreciate the fact that you don't have to stay awake and tell your body to breathe for you, or tell your heart to pump. Appreciate how wonderful that warm shower feels!

Appreciate the sunrise or sunset you may have enjoyed. Appreciate the planets for staying balanced within the solar system. Appreciate the pet that loves you unconditionally.

Appreciate positive aspects about what is going right in your life and the people you love.

Once you start finding things to appreciate, sometimes you get on a roll and can hardly stop! The momentum of your happy thoughts is creating expansion with the Law of Attraction which will continue to bring you more and more things to appreciate. Awesome, right?!

It's a whole lot easier to wake up with happy thoughts of a great day when you've gone to bed with a list of happy thoughts running through your mind the night before.

I suppose you could make other plans…but, why?!

Now, you could have made plans to have a crappy day, and that is certainly your choice. But, why?! Why would you want to go through the day feeling that bad? One note about the Law of Attraction, if you do wake up and start thinking about all the crappy things that happened yesterday, the momentum you are building in a negative thought pattern will continue AND expand!

I don't ever plan to have a crappy day - it just happens! I can't help that.

I'm clipping along just fine and then I spilled my coffee, smashed my finger in the door, and lost that important email! That's not my fault for having a crappy day!

Oh, believe me, I get it! When it rains, it pours. But, we can take our umbrella!

What the hell is that supposed to mean?

Let me explain. It has a lot to do with setting our intentions. Intentions are you, planning to set your energy in a high vibrational place! Of course, we don't *want* to have a bad day but if we don't make it a point to *intentionally* practice some gratitude before we go to bed and as soon as we wake up, we could get caught up in the thoughts of yesterday which may have not ended so well.

So, we get up and more crappy thoughts come in for us to think about. That's the momentum I was talking about. Once you start thinking a few negative thoughts, the Universe will match your thoughts with more that feel about the same or worse. Then, more and more things go wrong during the day, so you've basically made other plans - you just let the day hit you in the face.

That's why you've got to nip it in the bud! If you wake up and notice your thoughts don't feel very good, you are at a crossroads. You can choose to take crappy-thoughts-boulevard or you can decide to take the happy-highway.

So, I hope you choose the happy-highway and expand from there into a great day!

Here are the how-tos:

- Go to bed with an attitude of gratitude.
- As you lay in bed, set your intention that you're going to

wake up feeling good, refreshed, and in gratitude.

- As you fall asleep, make lists of things you appreciate.

- As you wake up, lay there for a few moments and renew your thoughts and feelings of gratitude, joy, and appreciation. Revel in the satisfying feeling of enjoying a great day!

We have so much to appreciate, how can you not be happy–at least sometime during each and every day if you're setting this kind of intention the night before and in the morning?!

I remember a conversation with my bonus daughter when she was 24-years-old and an ICU nurse. She said, *"It's always a good day! It might be a bad 10 minutes, but it's always a good day!"*

Don't you just love that attitude? Now, you *know* she's seen some bad shit that could make for a really bad day if she let herself go in that direction. But, she only *plans* to have a good day, no matter what!

Have a great day...and don't make any other plans!

Integrative Exercises

Use the following writing prompts this week to help you integrate what you've learned for your transformation.

Do you plan to have a great day? How have you done it up to this point?

How do you handle it when you start to have a great day and then shit hits the fan? Does the rest of your day roll downhill?

How do you return to your great day?

The steps for planning for a great day:

- Go to bed with an attitude of gratitude.

- As you lay in bed, set your intention that you're going to wake up feeling good, refreshed, and in gratitude.

- As you fall asleep, make lists of things you appreciate.

- As you wake up, lay there for a few moments and renew your thoughts and feelings of gratitude, joy, and appreciation. Revel in the satisfying feeling of enjoying a great day!

Practice this process all week! Journal about how well it went and if you made progress, celebrate! If it didn't go so well, how can you make improvements to your planning? Each day is a new day to plan for having a great day!

Chapter 11

Your Goal? Feel Good!

"If you had one goal, and that was to feel good, you would never again need to hear another word from anyone. You would live successfully and happily and in a way of fulfilling your life's purpose ever after."
~Abraham-Hicks

Just imagine! If we could all just make feeling good our number one goal in life, we could live happily ever after!

What does feeling good look like to you?

What would your life be like if you felt good most of the time?

What would you be, do, and have as a result of making feeling good your number one goal?

Let's talk about what a goal like feeling good looks like.

This is what MY goal to feel good would look like. Maybe some of it will resonate with you. If not, use my examples as your jumping-off place to create your own vision of what a life of feeling good would look like!

I would love life even more! I would experience more joy every single day!

Even when shit hits the fan, I would appreciate that the contrast I was experiencing was valuable in that I would get to choose what I do want because I'm seeing what I don't want.

I can appreciate the moments of feeling bad because I absolutely know my emotional guidance system is working well and indicating the direction I'm heading. So, I can choose which way to go next.

I can nip in the bud any doubt or fear because I easily notice when I'm feeling the discomfort of not knowing, thinking, and feeling like my Inner Being.

In those doubtful or fearful moments, I can laugh and acknowledge that they are not necessary thoughts! I can immediately shift my thinking and tell my new feel-good story. The more I tell the good-feeling story of my joyous life, the more I will begin to believe it! We believe what we repeat.

Feeling good indicates my alignment with who I really am as an extension of Source Energy.

I would feel the harmony of the wholeness of who I am as the physical-me and the spirit-me.

I would have amazing things arriving in my life experience on a daily basis.

I would feel so satisfied with everything and everyone.

Yet, even in my feelings of satisfaction, I'd know there would be so much more out there for me to explore. create, and receive! This makes me eager for more.

I would have perfect timing. I would meet the right people at the perfect time. I would say the right things. I would be in the right place at the right time which would lead me to something wonderful.

I would expect good things to come to me as quickly as I'm ready to receive them.

I would let everyone else off the hook, knowing that only I am responsible for feeling good. No others are necessary to my happiness and joy.

I would not feel the need to be in control of everyone or every situation around me.

I would feel safe, secure, assured, invincible, confident, clear-minded.

I would make decisions easily, knowing there is no risk, ever.

I would love everyone unconditionally – never demanding a changed behavior from anyone I observe so that I feel better. I would allow them to be who they are and respect their choices.

I would have doors and opportunities opening up for me from which to pick and choose.

I would have the best relationships; deep and enriching, fun and exciting.

I would experience peace and calm in my mind and soul.

I would look for everything that pleased me.

I would look for more things I wanted to be, do, and have.

My finances would be abundant. My bank accounts would reflect my abundant happiness.

My health would be fantastic. I would feel really good, physically. I would be strong, flexible, and at my naturally happy weight.

I would be living with very little resistance, so my discomfort level would be greatly diminished.

My beliefs would change into ones that were for my highest good, that would match my desires, that are calling Life Force through me.

I would feel my expansion and growth and be eager for what's coming next!

In this listing of what my goal of feeling good would look like, I chose more general statements of good feelings. It's imperative for us to get feeling good in general before we move into the specifics of feeling good. This gets our momentum going steadily before we add more specific details.

Once we are feeling really good, that's when we know we are aligned with our Inner Being (who we really are). In these moments, that's the time to move into more specific thoughts about what we want.

It's always your goal to steadily feel good before adding any specifics so they don't throw you out of alignment by introducing any resistance.

Don't let your thoughts about your desires and what you want to get out ahead of your alignment of feeling good. If you prematurely address your desires before you've created a vibrational environment to receive, you will introduce resistance that will slow down your process of receiving.

If you notice that what you want is still not there, that splits your energy away from feeling good. You'll notice that all too familiar twinge of frustration, disappointment, or doubt creep in. If this happens, just return to more general thoughts and leave the details until another time.

Stay focused on what makes you feel good. Notice throughout the day if what you're thinking feels satisfying or feels unsatisfying. At the moment you feel any dissatisfaction, change the subject to something that easily brings you the feeling of satisfaction.

Why does it even matter if we have a goal of feeling good?

Feeling good is a vibrational quality that matches your desires. Everything you want is vibrating at a good-feeling energy level. If you can achieve feeling good most of the time, you will shift your vibrational offering to such that the Universe must yield to you everything you desire. Not all at once, of course. We don't eat everything we want for a lifetime in one sitting. We don't breathe in all the air we will need for the rest of our lives. We want our desires to come at the perfect time over our lifetime.

We receive nourishment and air as we need it – as we're ready for more. The same goes in the Universe. We get to enjoy blessings all along the way. As we live a life of appreciation and focus on what's going right that feels good, we are well on our way to receiving our desires that create a really joyous life experience!

We came into this time-space-reality to experience as much joy as possible. The more you choose the goal to feel good, the more you will experience real joy!

Integrative Exercises

Use the following writing prompts this week to help you integrate what you've learned for your transformation.

What would feeling good look like to you? Write your description of your feeling-good state of being like I did in the example in the lesson.

What would your life be like if you felt good most of the time? Describe how your life would be different - improved - by feeling good most of the time.

What would you be, do, and have as a result of making feeling good your number one goal?

How could feeling good improve your relationships, health, finances, work, and spirituality? Write about each topic and how it could be improved if you really felt good. Even if you're not feeling good right now, can you write about your dream life of feeling good and what might be possible for you to experience? Use your imagination and dream big about living a life of joy, then, bask in the delight of your new vision! Wrap it around you like a cloak and revel in the exquisite feeling of simply feeling good now. Don't allow doubt to creep in. Remember, this is creating your reality as you feel good and dream, right here, right now!

Chapter 12

Feel Better First!

You want things because you believe that having them will make you feel better. Feel better first! Then they will come to you!

We all want things! Good things. No, *great* things!

This is natural and it is an eternal facet of our lives. Do you realize you were created to have desires? Making preferences of what we want is one of the main reasons we came into this time-space reality from the non-physical realm.

The wanting and desiring things actually expand all of creation! Being on the leading edge of thought allows us so many opportunities to see things in the world and then choose our preferences.

The contrast and variety of life offer us endless possibilities of desires!

This choosing process is what expands, not only our lives, it expands All-That-Is! Since we are eternal beings, we can't help but expand. Change is inevitable. Choices are required. But, it should never be a burden to make our choices. We should be approaching our preferences with joy!

When we see things in this world that we don't like, we immediately know what we do like - what would make us feel better. We make preferences all day, every day. Small choices and some we would consider huge. We ask for improvements by choosing our desired preferences.

When we make our preferences known to the Universe by our vibrational thoughts and their attached emotional expression, the Universe immediately goes in search of matching vibrations. This is the attraction factor in the Universe – otherwise known as the Law of Attraction – *that which is like unto itself is drawn.*

The longer we think and feel good about what we want, and if we are offering no resistance along the way (doubt, worry, fear, disappointment, etc), the Universe will bring it to us. This is the key: no resistance!

If you make a preference, Source understands your request, answers, YES, and then goes to work gathering all the cooperative components to make it happen. It is almost complete in the hands of Source, just waiting for us to be in the receiving mode.

So, what is the receiving mode? How do we get there?

The receiving mode feels amazing! It's exciting, exhilarating, and with an expectation of more. It's calm and relaxed. There is no resistance toward what we want. The pipeline is flowing freely. We allow Source to flow everything to us that we are ready for.

Everything we want is gestating in perfect timing awaiting our receptivity.

The receiving mode is the essence of how Source feels all the time. So, how does Source feel? You can know how Source feels when you experience the emotion of joy, love, appreciation, freedom, clarity, well-being, abundance, safety, excitement, exhilaration, eagerness, satisfaction. When you experience these high vibrational emotions and states of being, you are purely aligned with your Inner Source.

And, alignment is the receiving mode! Everything we want feels good and as we match those feelings, our beliefs and desires match and can easily flow into our lives.

What do I mean by resistance?

Resistance could be anything from twinges of doubt that we will actually get what we want, to full-blown feelings of unworthiness. Resistance is us doing things that disallow what we want and be who we truly are. It is really split energy.

On the one hand, we *know* what we want, we've asked for it and Source has answered affirmatively. So, we know it's in good hands and being tended to. On the other hand, we may begin doubting we will get it. We may get frustrated that it isn't coming. We see other people getting that thing we want so badly and ours hasn't come.

We may start complaining to someone or justify why we should get it. We start begging and pleading for it because it's getting serious! Now, we NEED it! With this resistant vibration, it is getting further away from us and slowing the process way down.

This is split energy that is confusing the universe in its job. You are giving the universe mixed signals. By law, the universe will give you everything you focus your dominant thoughts on. And, while you may be *thinking* you are simply thinking about what you want, you are, in reality, thinking about the *lack* of what you want. You are noticing what-is – and in your current condition with it missing.

With all this asking and then resisting, the universe is giving you some of each! Wanted and unwanted. Wanted or lack of what is wanted.

Get clear about what you want and why.

Your message must be clear about what you want and why. The how, when, where, and who are absolutely none of your business. That is the business of Source who is tending to your request. When we venture into Source's business of the how, when, where, and who, we are throwing resistance on our path because we don't have those answers. Then, what we want is slowed way down!

Your simple job in creating your reality is to decide what you want and why. The why just helps you fill in the details of how wonderful you will feel when you receive your desire. It's where you focus on the pleasures of having your desire. It's imagining the desire and the joys and good feelings you will experience when you receive it.

Just think about what you want for a moment. How good does that feel? *Why* you want it is to feel free, joyous, happy, expansive, supported, appreciative. You will feel loved, cherished, accomplished, confident. You will feel peaceful, calm, excited, and abundant. See, we did all that work and there is no resistance in any of those emotions or positive states of being. That's exactly where you need to be to receive what you want!

You must feel better first!

You must feel better BEFORE you can receive what you want. You can't think, *Well, when I get that, I'll be happy, I'll feel better*. That kind of thinking will only get you more lack of what you want. It will hold that wonderful thing away from your reach.

Feeling better must always precede the receiving of what you want!

Make lists of positive aspects about having this wonderful thing. Write lists and lists of the amazing feelings that you will experience. Imagine having it now! Write it in the present tense.

Here's a secret. The universe doesn't know the difference between imagination and reality. The universe doesn't know the difference between *imagining* that you have it and feeling how awesome you'll feel and if you actually feel really good *because* you already have it! All the universe is considering is your FEELING about your desire. The more you can feel amazing while imagining having your goodie, the Universe thinks you must already have it, so it runs out and brings it to you! By law, it has to make it happen - and quick!

So, feel better first! Practice the *feeling* of having what you desire NOW. Even before anything changes. You know it will make you feel really good when you do receive it, so take the plunge and feel better now. Make yourself feel as if it already exists in your hands. It does already exist in your vibrational escrow account. Source is tending to its details and growth. Waiting for you to feel better NOW!

And, it's a whole lot easier to feel good, really good, when you reawaken the joy within you - it IS who you really are!

WE ARE JOY!

Integrative Exercises

Use the following writing prompts this week to help you integrate what you've learned for your transformation.

Focusing on your WHY to Feel Better First!

Think about something you really want that hasn't come yet. In your journal, write down what it is at the top of a page. Under that, write your WHY. Only write about your WHY using good-feeling emotionally descriptive words that you feel deeply. And, add positive states of being that would support you in feeling really good right now as you write. Do this exercise every day this week. Below is an example from my life to give you an idea of how it looks.

At the top of my journal page, I would write:

I want a powerful new truck and luxurious camper because I want to hit the road with my Hubby and be self-contained to work from anywhere!

Then, I ask myself: Why do I want this? What is the deeper, *emotional* reason I want this? What does that *feel* like at my core? What feeling-state am I really wanting to accomplish?

It feels like freedom! And, freedom feels like...choices, options, possibilities, confidence. Freedom feels like abundance, fun, playfulness, laughter, and good humor. Freedom feels like clarity, support from the universe, happiness, adventure, and excitement. Freedom feels like peace, calm, ease, and flow.

Then I keep adding really good-feeling words that describe *how* my WHY *feels* to me! I repeat words or states of being when they really resonate with how I want to feel about what I want.

Don't get wrapped up in the details of why you want it from the standpoint of conditions because that can introduce resistance if you notice you don't have what you want! So, in my example I would NOT write:

It feels like freedom! And, freedom feels like traveling to new places, meeting new friends, seeing new vistas, working from anyplace we decide to camp. Freedom feels like sleeping in a luxurious camper in the mountains, watching beautiful sunrises and sunsets, and eating new local foods.

Don't focus on details of a *condition,* because in my situation, I could very easily slip into resistance because I may notice that I'm not experiencing those conditions, YET!

There's no resistance in simply expressing your WHY by how you want to FEEL!! That is the key to raising your vibration to FEEL BETTER FIRST to ALLOW the joy of things and conditions becoming what you desire! Feeling better first is what attracts the things you desire and deserve. Feeling better, feeling good is the first manifestation of your desire before it manifests into your reality!

About Mary Ann Pack

As a spiritual medium, owner of Envision Greatness LLC, and joy advocate, Mary Ann Pack guides women through a transformation to disrupt the patterns of pain and struggle, reawakening the joy within them. Mary Ann suffered religious trauma and, after leaving the church years ago, she has since thrived in joy, peace, and love. Today, she supports women on their quest to become their own sovereign!

Mary Ann's purpose in writing this book series is not only to help readers find their joy, their intuition, and their intention but also to guide their empowerment to understand that everyone is joy embodied since we are here to experience as much joy as possible.

Mary Ann began her wellness journey in 1993 when she sought to restore her own health. She earned a biblical studies degree and then later Practitioner's Certifications in Psych-K and Law of Attraction. She has extensively studied energy work and holistic healing practices. In 2014, Mary Ann received her Life Coaching Certification from Life Mastery Institute.

When Mary Ann is not studying, writing her growing book series, running her spiritual groups, or coaching, she loves to share her joy and wisdom with her husband, their blended family, and grandchildren.

www.MaryAnnPack.com

About Envision Greatness Press

Envision Greatness Press is a subsidiary of Envision Greatness, LLC. Mary Ann Pack and her husband, Randall, started their company to create coaching opportunities for those on a quest for more from life.

As the managing member, Mary Ann, has broadened the mission of the company to include her long-held vision of publishing books for transforming the lives of her readers.

When Mary Ann received the idea for this book series, she knew it was time to create a publishing imprint of her own. So, working with a publishing expert was required. She found the support and training she needed by working with Elizabeth B. Hill of Green Heart Living.

This series of books entitled, *We Are Joy!* will each contain 12 lessons with integrative exercises to help readers assimilate all that they are learning for a transformational experience. Each book will address a different topic for readers' growth and evolution. A members-only book club is available to study each book as they are published with coaching and live Q&A sessions.

Envision Greatness Press will be accepting authors who are interested in being published. If you have a book idea or want to consult with Mary Ann about publishing your writings, please contact her via email at wecare@wearejoybooks.com

Coming in This Series

We Are Joy! Spirit Guide Messages

We Are Joy! Sacred Crystals

We Are Joy! Unmuted Voices

We Are Joy! Thriving Beyond Indoctrinated Trauma

We Are Joy! Loving Relationships

We Are Joy! Animal and Nature Spirits

We Are Joy! Joyous Service

We Are Joy! My Body, My Partner

www.WeAreJoyBooks.com

Made in the USA
Columbia, SC
27 January 2022